Steel Whe

and

Rubber Tyres

Volume Four

A General Manager's Journey
Whitehall
Aberdare
Drawlane Group
Leicester
Oldham

by

Geoffrey Hilditch

OBE, Ch Eng, FI Mech E, FILT, FCIT, MIRTE

Venture *publications*

© 2017 Venture Publications Ltd

ISBN 978 1905 304 813

City Flyer — A Leicester City Transport Leyland Leopard is seen here laying over at Halifax bus station on the City Flyer service, described in the previous volume. This service linked Blackpool with Dover via Halifax and Leicester. GG Hilditch became involved near to the end of his days as General Manager at Leicester. After some ten years since leaving Halifax, Mr Hilditch ran buses and coaches in Halifax again!

CONTENTS

The author is seen here in 1984, together with his wife Muriel, daughter Diane, and son Christopher, after receiving his OBE at Buckingham Palace, awarded for his work pioneering the first bus service for disabled people in Leicester.

Publisher's Preface

Geoffrey Hilditch's career in municipal transport meant he was never far away from the influence of politicians, local or national. As we saw in Volume 3, left-winger Barbara Castle upset his applecart in Halifax and the PTAs which her Transport Act created were completely unpalatable to him.

The opportunity to get back to being the 'main man' as a municipal manager – in Leicester this time – seemed to have the potential to turn the clock back nicely when he took that position in October 1975. How wrong can you be?

All was well at first, and his relationship with Dennis Brothers will forever be remembered as almost certainly being the saviour of that concern, but in a period of ever-increasing costs – in 1980/1, for example, platform staff were awarded a national increase of 13%, adding to many other burdens such as rising fuel and new vehicle prices over which the industry had no control – the halcyon days of showing a good profit became very much a thing of the past.

Geoffrey's left-wing political masters – his Transport Committee – became increasingly dissatisfied and impatient with the situation and relationships soured whilst ridership declined and costs continued to increase until, eventually, he was offered early retirement in 1984 at the age of 59. This escape route was too attractive to ignore, and moving with his wife down to their spacious holiday home in Torbay seemed set to put a happy ending to the story.

Just days before finishing at Leicester – out of the blue – he took a phone call in his office which was to start him on yet another and completely unexpected career. After initially working with national politicians and the judicial system in Whitehall he found himself getting involved in and then out of some of the more adventurous aspects of the post-deregulation world he had been called to advise on. Be careful what you wish for.

If red-Barbara had upset his and the rest of the industry's applecart whilst he was in Halifax it was as nothing to compare with the escapades in the industry post blue-Nicholas, as touched upon in this Volume. Some of his colleagues sailed too close to the wind of change and paid the price . . . Geoffrey was wiser and more careful.

Sadly he did not live to see the story of the end of his career make it into print, but we are pleased to be able to record the final part of his autobiography, to look back in admiration at his determination not to be thwarted by British Leyland, and to have had the pleasure of working with a remarkable man.

1 – Wanderings in Whitehall

As no one at Leicester had asked me had I any outstanding holidays due to me, I did my own assessment and came to the conclusion that my service with LCT could legitimately end on Wednesday 22nd August 1984, so on that morning I went to the office as usual and worked away quietly doing what I had to do.

At lunch time I went to Rutland Street in order to entertain my guest, Traffic Commissioner Mr Ken Peter. We had a meal and a chat and I told him that I would be moving very quickly to Torbay, so gave him my address and phone number. He wished me good fortune in the future, and after he had left I returned to Abbey Park Road and waited for the arrival of my afternoon tea. I then asked three of the Chief Officers to join me, when I told them that in a very few minutes I would be departing for retirement, saying that I would like to shake them by the hand and thank them for the support they had given me over the years. I indicated that I was choosing this sudden method of departure because I did not want to be involved in any retirement gatherings, possible presentations etc, so I left them with something to talk about and then went for a quick walk around the garage to say goodbye to various staff members. However, when I returned to my car, which was near the office, several staff members were standing by it, and extended their good wishes to me.

I drove out of the gates, thinking as I did so that this was the end of my transport career, and I found myself quite looking forward to starting a new life in the Devon sun, but with a two-day-a week job to help keep me amused should I begin to suffer from boredom. Little did I know what would be coming.

A hectic morning followed, when our Scraptoft Lane house was put on the market. Then after lunch we loaded up the car and left for Torbay, to begin life there on a firm note by cutting the lawns. On the following Monday I surprised my wife by saying, "I am going to add a touch of class to the Job Centre this morning by going to it in the Daimler and signing on so I can draw the dole". As I shall only be working two days a week I might as well take what I am entitled to as I have paid the National Insurance charges now for some 30 years.

On arrival at that office, which was not far from home, a young male clerk began to interview me and so I explained my situation. That I had now retired from full time employment, was still under 60, and in a few days would start a two-day-a week part-time job, but I did not say where that job was and, surprisingly, he did not ask for details. Then I became very amused.

My guide into what was a completely unknown world produced a set of forms, asked me the questions printed thereon, and filled in the answers as I provided them. He then came to ask me what my weekly wage had been, but I had to say I did not know. I had been paid on an annual basis but if he would produce a calculator, and then divide by 52 the figure I would say, he would have his answer. With the calculator at the ready I told him what the figure had been, when he said almost in awe "Oh sir, what a lot of money". From that moment on he began to treat me with quite unnecessary respect, which in a way was rather touching, but then Torbay is not and never has been a high wage area.

Some of the newest London Transport vehicles when I came to work in London were Leyland Titans and MCW Metrobuses. The upper view shows Metrobus M 753 (A753 THV) near to the Tower of London, operating a sightseeing tour. Nearby is Leyland Titan T 944 (A944 SYE) which is about to cross Tower Bridge on the route 78 to Dulwich.

During my time in Whitehall, Routemasters were still in everyday service. The above view shows one of the earliest, RM 6, on route 237. The lower picture shows RM 2147 waiting behind RM 577 in Knightsbridge, close to the Royal Albert Hall.

It seemed that with an allowance for my wife, I was due for a payment of around £56.00 per week, so I thanked him for his kind help and bade him good morning. Thereafter, each time that I went into the office, he always addressed me as "Sir", though do not assume here that I was unduly affluent. The Daimler was third-hand and had covered a pretty high mileage, looking better at first sight than it actually was. I will not repeat what my wife said when I made my quip about taking the car to the Job Centre, but I assure you that it was both crisp and pithy. In such a manner did my apparent retirement begin, but retirement was much further away than I could ever have realised hence the ongoing size of this publication.

Consequently, on 30th August 1984, I journeyed to Marsham Street as a prospective employee for the very first time, and duly reported to the Under Secretary, Mr AP Brown, responsible for doing what the Civil Service had to do: to bring the Transport Bill into law. I was told that a sum of money had been placed against my name – this being my budget – and from it I would draw my salary and my legitimate expenses. We went over the attendant situation as it then was, and I was introduced to those members of the team that I had yet to meet. The day passed very quickly and then I made my way to the hotel where I had reserved accommodation for the night.

Now it can be said that there are two parts to the process in which I had now become involved. Firstly conversion, ie the conversion of a White or Green Government paper into an Act of Parliament, and then the process of implementation of this new law. At this time the Department was immersed in the conversion part. I now discovered, rather to my surprise, that I was to go as a Department Representative to the various conferences, much like as in my day as a General Manager. The end of the month saw me in Blackpool for the Confederation's annual gathering, and if I was surprised to be there some of my former colleagues were more surprised than I was!

Before this event took place though I had a separate trip to London to take part in what I firmly expected would be my last meetings of the Employer's Federation and the National Joint Industrial Counci (NJIC), and after submitting my resignation from the former, I received as a parting gift for my past efforts an 00-gauge model of an ex-Lancashire and Yorkshire Railway 4-6-0 passenger locomotive. This was finished in BR livery as the last survivor of its class. It is still to be seen running on my extensive layout being a very excellent performer. How wrong can you be?

I continued to spend up to two days a week at the Department, but my journeys to the Job Centre came to a rapid end. Nevertheless, before this event took place, my friendly contact at that establishment truly marvelled when I told him of my new commitment "In Whitehall too". My rapid severance, however, was due to two more totally unexpected offers.

I had previously engaged a then well-known firm of experts to deal with my tax affairs, so now I was earning an income once more I had to supply them with the details. It then transpired that the consultancy arm of the business were offering to guide bus operators through the legislative minefield that was awaiting them, so as I would have to be learning all about the contents of the Bill, perhaps I would assist the firm and its clients in so far as I was able. However, I had to bear in mind the fact that I had signed the Official Secrets Act, and some of the information that would come into my possession could not be revealed to outside parties. A second such company then heard of my association with the first, and it too asked if I could possibly help in a similar way, so in no time at all my two days a week in Marsham Street turned into five, or another two or three when I visited the headquarters of these consultants, or at times I went with their staff members to visit their clients and spread the word. But at this point let us return to Marsham Street.

The offices of the Department possessed no architectural merit whatsoever. The building consisted of a low main block that ran the whole length of the site. This was some four storeys in height, the ground floor possessing a full-length reception area with an entrance door at each end. Each of these was guarded by a security office and the attendant staffs, so to gain access you either produced your pass or stated your business and were then usually allowed to take a seat, where one remained under the scrutiny of the security staff.

They would phone who it was that one was to see, and so a staff member would come down from the upper-regions to escort you to your desired location. The words upper-regions are here entirely appropriate. From the base block sprouted three tower blocks with, if I recall correctly, each of some 16 floors. Escalators gave access to each of the main block floors above reception, but if you wanted to reach floor number five, or those higher, then one had to resort to the lifts which were an experience in themselves. Reputed to be the second fastest in Europe, ongoing up you stepped into one of the set located at either end of reception, pressed the button, there was then a 'swoosh', and you stepped out at your destination which in the case of the Bill team was floor number 13. That, though, was going up. Coming down was another matter altogether, and I sometimes felt that after a downwards trip my stomach and my body were not connected again until I had walked some way along Marsham Street. Alas, escalators to floor four, and then eight flights of steps, was not a realistic option to high speed vertical travel. At the time of my arrival their reliability record was not of the highest order until, so we were told, a posse of very VIPs became trapped in one, when rapid maintenance activity became the order of the day.

Now it was also reputed that the site had been previously occupied by a gas works, which some unkind people might think was very appropriate, but be that as it may. It was also suggested that the design had been undertaken by the Office of Works, fresh from the triumph of completing a prison. Certainly the long corridors running along the lengths of the towers with their numerous office doors did give one the impression of being in a house of confinement. Go through a door though, and one could tell instantly of the importance of the occupant. Lesser mortals had no carpet, no framed pictures and no curtains. They had though, like all other occupants, a magnificent view of London where from floor 13 you looked down on the birds, and could almost shake hands with the pilots of jets heading for Heathrow. The number of windows between the partition walls was another indication as to the rank of the occupant, where wooden furniture would replace steel, and the whole ambiance was of enhanced comfort. It was to a stranger like myself all very interesting, so more introductions soon followed, and from then on I found that without exception the staff members that formed the Bill team were both friendly and at all times helpful.

I discovered that when thoughts of a new Transport Act began to circulate in Whitehall, a select band of Civil Servants had gone into a huddle and produced a goodly number of papers on all the subjects that would seem to be pertinent to arriving at the end result. These covered, for example: taxi licensing; Traffic Commissioners; Road Service licensing; the role of the National Bus Company in the scheme of things; and the possible future of the Passenger Transport Executives. I was presented with copies of these to read and digest, so initially my time would be fully occupied.

After the authors had digested, amended and condensed these papers as appeared desirable, and the senior members of the gang had written their version of a possible White Paper, and I use the words 'their version' advisedly as this was written in the English that we simple mortals could understand.

This was not though the end of the story, but before we go any further note the colour. If the end result is a White Paper it signifies that the Government has a working majority, and this is its firm intention. If it is a Green Paper then here is a possible intention, but as a Government we are open to suggestions. Here the Transport Paper was reputedly White – with a few Green edges – but at this point I refrain from further comment.

Well, that White Paper was certainly being discussed before I left my Leicester office, and, both in that City and within the Association of District Councils transport bodies, it could be truthfully said that it was not being received with acclaim. This was quite the reverse in fact, but the process continued.

The White paper of July1984 was passed to the Parliamentary Council who occupy offices over Horse Guards Parade and they then rewrote the document in what I can only describe as Parliamentary Script. The sponsor was, of course, the Right Honourable Nicholas Ridley, MP, Secretary of State for Transport, being assisted by Mr David Mitchell, MP, Minister of State at the Department. These two gentlemen began to hold meetings with interested parties, to explain the intention behind the proposed legislation, and answer questions thereon, and there was certainly no shortage of these. It was, of course, suggested that the industry was in need of shaking up from its complacency, being protected from competition by the effects of Road Service Licensing. Throw the roads open to competition and there would be more choice for the passenger, fares could well be reduced and overall efficiency would be enhanced. Well, there might have been a modicum of truth in these assertions, but let's look a little bit further.

The Conservative Government was in the process of selling off various state-owned enterprises, and a whole series of these were at the time in the process of passing into private shareholding hands, so the intention to break up and then sell off the various subsidiaries of the National Bus Company and the Scottish Bus Group was certainly no surprise. Similarly, the Passenger Transport Executives were also to be involved. Their place in the scheme of things had been altered with the passing of quite recent legislation.

This totally eliminated the Metropolitan County Councils, and so automatically ended the lives of the then PTAs. Their place had been taken by what was in effect a Joint Committee, members of which were drawn from the constituent local authorities. Now it was intended to break up the PTE bus undertakings, and to place them at arm's-length from their quite new authorities. But despite all this, why involve the remaining and quite independent separate Council controlled bus undertakings? At first sight one would have thought that they could carry on as of yore – but perhaps, on second thought, the answer must be in the negative. If competition was going to be the name of the game, then steps had to be taken to ensure these undertakings entered the real world, and so would not be able to be supported by the general rate fund if they should run into financial difficultly. However, were there any other attendant considerations? As a municipal service, a municipal bus undertaking was not ever called upon to pay income tax, but as an independent company it would be. Additionally, we hear a lot these days about the costs to the community at large of the funding of the Local Government Superannuation Scheme. Undertaking employees of all ranks were invariably members of this, but what would their situation be in the future?

Consequently, many questions came to be asked, but as was only to be expected in these early stages. However, fully informative answers were all too often not forthcoming. Nevertheless, I had asked one all-important question before I said "yes" to the offer made to me by the Under Secretary, who suggested that I might join the Department of Transport as the Government's Bus Operations Advisor. The question was, "Is this part of a scheme to ensure the ending of local municipal bus undertakings?" The answer I was given was a very positive "No", and I never saw anything in my time in Marsham Street to suggest that this was not the truth. It is true that since Deregulation Day one might think that all-too-many have disappeared, but there would seem to be two basic reasons for this. Some time down the track, cash-strapped Councils realised that they had a saleable asset ready to hand, and in any event, members of the owning Council did not have the influence and interest in operations that they had in the Good Old Committee days. Consequently, sales began to be very frequent. Then just a few failed because their small size was unable to fend off the competition from the large local private concerns that soon came their way. One might suggest that the undertakings at Darlington, Lancaster and Barrow suffered in this way, and then in my view some failures occurred because the base upon which they were set up was not just as firm as it might have been. I remember in the early days going to an undertaking where controversy reigned, the Union blaming the Management for not preparing properly for impending deregulation, and the Members of the Transport Committee blaming the Unions for non co-operation. It was a high cost operation unit and quite obviously if it was going to survive in the new world then the search for economy had to begin forthwith.

As I had been asked for my advice I gave it, when the Chairman held up his hands in horror and said it was against his socialist principles to do what I was suggesting. I asked if it was also against those principles to make the staff redundant, as would inevitably be the case if the nettle was not grasped and grasped very quickly. I did not receive a reply, and I will leave you, reader, to guess the end result. In the meantime things had been marching on.

The so-called White Paper with green edges entitled 'Buses', as Command 9300 had cost £5.85 to buy and for your money you obtained eight chapters, three annex and 79 pages, but this document had been turned into that first draft of the Transport Bill. Now we had pages, clauses, and a series of schedules, whilst at the end was a list of those parts of the existing legislation that would be repealed once this new Bill became law.

I no longer have a copy of this document in my possession, but a later edition that remains in my files is made up of 173 pages, 13 clauses and a series of schedules. There was certainly no shortage of reading material for those of us who were involved in all this at the time. By this time my engagement had been subject to some change. This process began one Monday morning when I indicated to our Under Secretary that I did not suppose I would be seeing him after the end of the week. He queried this statement, so I told him that I had been doing some arithmetic, and found that my initial budget would by Friday have been entirely spent. He digested this news and promptly left the office, to return a wee while later to provide me with an increased figure, at the same time saying that from now on I had better be available for three days per week instead of two, but it was not long before three days became five. This meant that my association with the two Consultancy firms had come to an end, but this must have occurred in any event as it was simply not compatible with my Department engagement.

Once the draft Bill had been published, the next stage in its metamorphosis was to make it into an Act of Parliament, which was then put into motion. Firstly the Bill was laid before the House of Commons for its technical first reading, and it was interesting here to look inside the front cover of the document and read the list of its sponsors. Thereafter it was remitted to the Bill Committee for detailed consideration, where I began to attend the meetings of this body as and when they took place. The Speaker of the House appointed the Chairperson of the Committee, namely Betty Boothroyd MP, who later on was elected Speaker of the House in her own right. Then the political parties nominated their members who were to serve thereon and so now the debate on the contents of the Bill could begin. The building that houses the House of Commons contains several Committee rooms on the upper floors, which are in effect mini parliamentary chambers.

At one end of these chambers is a platform on which sits the Chairman, together with the Clerk to the Committee and other supporting officials. At right angles to the platform are the seats for the members, with the supporters of the Government sitting to the right hand side of the Chair, the opposition to the left. At the far end of those member's seats or benches is the bar of the room marked with a white line which no unauthorised person must pass, and beyond the bar facing the platform are the seats for the public should any one want to hear what is going on in Committee.

The leader of the Government side, who is leading the case for turning the Bill into law, sits as close to the Chair as possible, at the platform end of his side are benches with his second in command next to him (or her, of course). Hard by the Leader is the so-called 'box'. This is at main floor level and situated as close to the Leader as possible. Here sit the higher Bill team Civil Servants, positioned so that they can quickly provide the Leader with any information that he might want, and also become aware of how the passage of the Bill through Committee is proceeding. This was where I had to sit, with my confreres.

Each committee room had two doors, each being guarded by an Official of the House garbed in the requisite attire. The door nearest to the platform was the one used by the Members of Parliament and officials; the one at the other end was for the use of visitors or the press. Committee sessions started each morning at around ten o'clock, when the Chair would open the proceedings to start them off from the place where termination had occurred at the end of the previous session, but this was always at the end of a clause. Consequently, if discussion ceased on completion of clause 31 yesterday, we began today to consider clause 32.

The Leader would spell out what a wonderful thing was being proposed here. It would rejuvenate what had become an unfortunate situation, and so be of great benefit to both the industry and its passengers. The opposition would then come in, in this particular case being spearheaded by the late Mrs Gwyneth Dunwoodie MP, who might well declare that this was a lot of pure rubbish and would do much more harm than good. Then those members who wished to have their say would join in, and so the debate ranged from one side of the room to the other and across the space separating those two sets of benches. Oft times a consensus would be reached and so the Committee passed on to deal with the next clause, but on quite a number of occasions the request was made for a division when the requisite procedure had to be followed. The Chair would say, "We will have a division", and the guardians of the doors would go into the corridor and call loudly "Division in number Three", or whatever the room number happened to be, whilst the TV monitors positioned all round the House of Commons would display that same information.

After a short pause to allow any Member who had gone out for some reason or other to regain his or her place, the Chair would say "Lock" and the two flunkeys would lock the doors so no further entry was possible. Those in favour of the clause would stand and as the Clerk read their names out would sit down once more, and then the opposition members would do likewise. The totals for and against would be recorded and the paper bearing the information was passed to the Chair, who would then proclaim, "The Ayes have it, the Ayes have it", or the no's of course if the vote had gone the other way.

The division now concluded, and the Chair would say "Unlock", and the flunkeys would employ their keys accordingly and the Committee would then proceed to cover the next clause. Some amendment did result from these processes but one thing was clear, the Government had the majority and by and large the main purposes as set out in the Bill were going to come to fruition. It was, though, all quite fascinating stuff and I had never ever in my wildest dreams thought that I would ever closely witness Parliament at work.

At this time though, that Committee was meeting twice per day with an evening session starting around 6.00pm, and so this meant a long day for those of us involved. One usually arrived at the office fairly early and went over the preceding day's events, looking over the revised copy of the Bill that incorporated any changes that had been made to it. At that time this revised version was printed overnight – a very fast service. The morning session of the Bill Committee then followed, going on to lunch time. After a suitable break for refreshment it was a return to the office until it was time to walk back to the House to listen to the Committee's evening sessions. These usually ended at a reasonable hour when it was possible to return to my chosen hotel for dinner, but

At the time of the visit to Derby Corporation, Barton Transport and NBC subsidiary Trent which has been merged with Midland General. The NBC concern was typically Bristol VRTs, a few Leyland Olympians along with Leyland Nationals. This view of Broadmarsh bus station in Nottingham reflects that mixture.

Some Trent vehicles were painted in Midland General livery to mark the 65th anniversary of that company in 1985. Bristol VRT with Eastern Coachworks body, FRB 211H, was one of the vehicles to wear this blue livery.

I have a note in my diary to that which took place on the 23rd of April, which did not end until 12.05am.

However, not every weekday was spent in London, and so from time to time I was able to visit various undertakings and discuss with my former managerial colleagues the finer points of the intended legislation and how it could come to affect them. Some of these trips took me into new territories. For example, on the 10th June 1985 I visited Barrow for the first time, on the 17th and 18th I was at Trent, Barton and Derby CT, a period when one of my contacts asked me if there would be any payment to offset the loss of his concerns, goodwill which he felt would be totally extinguished. There was no answer to that one.

The following week I was engaged similarly at Southdown, Brighton CT and Brighton and Hove. I half expected that my reception at the various NBC concerns would, to say the least, be frosty, for it had been rumoured that some concern had been expressed within that organisation that a long term ex-municipal General Manager had been given such a post, but with only one notable exception, I was always received with courtesy and friendliness.

As was to be expected, the Bill Committee continued with its deliberations and, in anticipation of the eventual outcome, I found myself over two days in September taking my place on a small panel set up to recruit two firms of consultants. One of these was intended to monitor the financial position at Deregulation Day of the various NBC concerns to make sure that they commenced life on 'an even playing field', the other firm was to do likewise covering the municipal and PTE bus units.

A sales organisation to market and obtain the best price possible for what would become the ex-NBC undertakings was also in the process of being brought into being, whilst consideration was being given as to how the larger units might be broken down into smaller businesses. I gathered that more of these than were actually set up could have been preferred, but the NBC headquarters – not unnaturally – did not display much enthusiasm for the idea, pleading that it had already begun to break up some of its companies (eg what had been Midland Red), and in any event there was not the staff available to do much more in the short time up to Deregulation Day.

I had an interesting time here, contemplating just what I would do if I had total personal powers – which I most certainly had not – to reconstitute the NBC business, but as all this was purely pie in the sky, I will not pursue the ideas any further, but with committee meetings, the office work load, and travel to far away places, the days passed quickly and very pleasantly. One such journey certainly caught me out though, thanks to a meeting scheduled for a Friday afternoon in Aberdeen of all places. My way home meant a train to Edinburgh, and then catching the 11.40pm sleeper from that City to Plymouth, having a bed for the night and alighting at Newton Abbot, there to board the branch line train for Torquay.

Only a few days later I was back in Scotland again, this time visiting Dundee and Glasgow, so I journeyed once more to Edinburgh and boarded the 11.40pm sleeper. I recall having a restful night, but awoke after we ran into Taunton and duly dressed. The ticket collector then appeared, snipped mine and made no comment about its Newton Abbot endorsement. Consequently, as we ran through Teignmouth I gathered my things together and stood in the corridor,

Among the towns visited during the period covered by this chapter were Barrow in Furness, Lancaster and Brighton. Barrow had bought a number of Leyland Atlanteans and, in 1984, purchased three Leyland Fleetlines from London Transport. Travelling along Abbey Road, passing the station, is No.101 (OJD 174R).

Prior to the local government changes in 1974, Lancaster had its own municipal buses, as did Morecambe and Heysham. These were merged to become the Lancaster City Council fleet. Coaches were not common in municipal fleets, but Lancaster ran a pair of Leyland Leopards with Duple bodies, which were purchased in 1979. Number 11 (URN 11V) is on the promenade at Morecambe.

The Souhdown fleet was noted for its large quantities of Leyland PD3s with Northern Counties bodywork, which were preferred to the rear-engined vehicles which entered service with most BET fleets. Thirty of these were fitted with convertible open-tops and remained in service even after the arrival in NBC days of Bristol VRT/ECW convertibles. One of the Southdown routes was from Eastbourne to Beachy Head, where No.411 (411 DCD) is seen.

Rear-engined vehicles arrived in Brighton with the Bristol VRTs for Southdown in early NBC days. Brighton Corporation bought Leyland Atlanteans from 1971 and this 1975 vehicle, with East Lancs dual-door body, No 54 (JFG 354N), is posed on Madeira Drive.

At the time of the author's visit to Aberdeen, the mainstay of the Grampian fleet were Alexander-bodied Leyland Atlanteans, originally chosen by Aberdeen Corporation. Following the Scottish local government changes of 1975, this operator became Grampian Regional Transport. The vehicles were always smartly turned out, as shown by this later view of No.226 in the post-deregulation livery in Union Street, Aberdeen.

Aberdeen was also the headquarters of Scottish Bus Group subsidiary W Alexander & Son (Northern) which also served the city and the rural area, as far as Inverness. ECW-bodied Daimler Fleetline, TGM 232J, is on Union Terrace with His Majesty's Theatre, Aberdeen in the background.

Dundee Corporation Transport had been renamed Tayside in 1975. The Bus and Coach Council was promoting the use of buses with 'We'd all miss the bus' special liveries which appeared in many fleets. The Alexander-bodied Ailsa is loading adjacent to the shopping centre in Dundee.

Glasgow Corporation had been succeeded by Strathclyde PTE and was still running a large fleet of Alexander-bodied Leyland Atlanteans. They had also tried the Ailsa and, as this view shows, Metrobuses, although in this case bodywork is by Alexander rather than MCW's own construction. EUS 106X had been new in February 1982.

ready to alight at my intended station, only – horrors – we swept through at quite a speed only to come to a sudden stop at Aller Junction. The frequent bus service to Paignton was only a few yards away, but leaving the train there was not possible so it was next stop Plymouth and make my way back to Newton Abbott as soon as possible. Moral, make sure you take due note of any timetable alterations before you board your chosen train. I didn't. If, however, one train would not stop for me another certainly had to.

I went off to visit several operators in the Liverpool/Wigan area and chose to travel by train. I stayed the night at the Haydock Post House, and consulted the timetable I always had with me. I found that there was a convenient morning train from Newton-le-Willows to Manchester that would give me nice time to cross to Piccadilly, and there pick up a London train that would have me back in Marsham Street in order to be present at a meeting convened by the Minister of State Mr David Mitchell MP.

I duly booked a taxi from the hotel to the station, went into the booking office and asked for a single to London. The booking clerk, with a resigned air, asked me was I wanting to catch the train I had initially selected, and when I answered in the affirmative he told me in flat tones that it had been cancelled but knew not why. I protested, told him that I worked for the Department of Transport and now thanks to British Rail's poor service would not be able to attend a meeting I was supposed to be at. Initially he was of the obvious opinion that here was another would-be passenger spinning a yarn, but when I showed him my Departmental pass his attitude changed. Excusing himself for a wee while he went into another part of the office and there made a phone call, but I could not hear what was said. On his return he said he had been on to control, and in the situation a Chester to Manchester express was going to make a special stop for me, an event that should take place in about 40 minutes. So as it was a cold morning, would I care to come into the booking office? I declined his invitation with thanks, saying that I had an aunt who lived just around the corner in Leigh Terrace. To her house I went, to receive a warm welcome that was reinforced with tea and cake.

On my return to the platform there was a short interlude, and then the signals came off and from the Earlestown direction came a longish train headed by a diesel locomotive. It swept to a halt, a porter opened the door to a first class carriage, the guard stepped out, saluted me and when I had boarded waved the train on its way – next stop Manchester. This was service with a capital 'S', but nothing of the sort has ever happened since and it is now very unlikely to do so ever again. Marsham Street certainly had its uses.

Eventually the Bill passed through all the requisite Parliamentary stages, and on the 30th October 1985 it received the signature of the Queen. Thus it became the 1985 Transport Act and the Bill team had a party at Marsham Street to celebrate the event. If, by the way, it had not been turned into law by the end of the current session of Parliament, the whole process would have to have started again – from the beginning – at the commencement of the next session, unless of course the Government should have a change of heart and decide to forget the whole intention.

Next our attention was turned to the implementation side of the business, everyone in the Industry now being fully aware that monumental changes were in the offing. The changes involved are far too numerous to catalogue here, but briefly within what was still the municipal world, Councils were giving thought to the company structure that was going to be called for, and who was going to be appointed to the Board of Directors. Here the Act made it plain that Executive Directors had to be in the full time service of the Company, which doubtlessly caused some heartburn in various breasts. Those who were nominated for executive roles had to be thinking about which services could be run commercially, and which should be laid at the doors of the new tendering authorities. At the same time, they had to try to forecast what competition might come to be experienced, and what effect it could have on the Business Plan that had to be formulated when in many cases undertakings recruited their own consultants to help put a plan together. Some of my former colleagues like Edward Deakin of Bradford, decided that this was all too much and being of the desired age applied for early retirement as he had said he would when we met in the previous volume. Believe me all this certainly caused a fluttering in management circles, when the size of the post-deregulation fleet had to be tailored to the demands that were going to be placed on it. From a Marsham Street point of view, theory had now to be turned into practice and so what were known internally as 'Road Shows' came into being.

A suitable fair-sized meeting room would be booked in some local hotel, and all the operators and tendering authorities in the area would be invited to come along, meet members of what had been the Bill team, listen to their exposition of the implications of the new act and ask whatever questions they might have in mind. Here I began to encounter another series of experiences, and not all were really to do with the actual business intended.

On occasions, Road Shows would be held on a Monday morning which meant travelling to the venue on Sunday when train travel could take on a new dimension, time keeping not being of a high order. Such experiences included travel from Bristol to Gloucester via Swindon, a train that took the wrong set of points and happily galloped towards York before the driver came to realise that this was not right, and when, after a long delay, we set back to the junction and so gained the right line. On another occasion, due to engineering work, we were diverted via Barnsley, only some entrepreneurs had stolen a length of signal cable not very long before we reached the associated area. I can tell you that a long term view of Barnsley by moonlight is far from romantic. These were external incidents though, and there were also one or two internal ones. Picture the scene. The dining car steward is about to serve hot tomato soup from a silver metal tureen. The driver fails to observe a 20mph restriction over a bridge that is under repair and must have crossed it at a speed in excess of 60mph. The train lurches widely, and that tomato soup is distributed far more widely than was ever intended as the steward loses his balance and heads towards the floor. Not, however, half as interesting as the occasion when I was joined at my table in the restaurant car by a very smartly attired lady of around thirty summers, who proceeded to tell me that she was returning to London after being the best man at a wedding. She had obviously had far too much to drink, but called for further bottles of wine which she insisted on sharing with me. Her behaviour then became totally uncontrollable so we had better leave further details from

During my visits to Scotland, I frequently changed trains in Edinburgh.Lothian had become the successor to Edinburgh Corporation Transport which had started to standardise on Leyland Atlanteans with Alexander bodies. Long-wheelbase Olympians then took over, as this later view in Princes Street demonstrates.

The London General Omnibus Co opened its bus maintenance facility on Chiswick High Road, which covered 32 acres, in 1921, which passed to London Transport in 1933. This photograph was taken some 50 years later when the works held a Golden Jubilee celebratory event. By this time the need for two works (the other being at Aldenham) was being called into question by the 'powers that be' and the result was my visit.

this record. Mind you, this was only part of the story. Where do you find a meal late on Sunday if BR has not provided one, in say downtown Thurso or Blackwood? We had some odd meals in odd places. All this though is an aside from the substance of this chapter so let us return to the main theme.

As Deregulation Day was scheduled for the 26th of October 1986, there was just under a year for everyone who was going to be affected by the legislation to do whatever they had to do, and so we became involved in ever-more meetings. Some of these meetings were productive, some not, whilst matters which needed to be settled were considered in detail and then solutions were found.

One such matter concerned those municipal employees who were members of the Local Government Superannuation Scheme, which was not going to include anyone who would find themselves in the service of one of the new companies. The sensible answer was the formulating of the so called 'Deeming Option', by which those paying their contributions to that scheme were transferred to a new company on the 26th, and could continue to do so and retain their membership. Any new starters after the 25th, however, would have to join whatever pension scheme might be instituted by the employer.

As this sort of ongoing review continued, the weeks sped by and I began to wonder what I would do when my work at Marsham Street came to an end as it inevitably must. However, with travel, office work, and the reading of business plans that began to appear in the office, there was not much time to dwell on that aspect of the matter.

In this period came a very surprising interruption when I was asked to go and look over the Chiswick works of London Transport, and submit my observations thereon. I went to the works in December and spent a day going around the premises which were certainly extensive. It seemed that my appearance provoked some unease amongst the representatives of the workforce, as much of the plant seemed to have been out of use for quite some time, a state of affairs that certainly applied in the well-equipped machine shops where a high proportion of the lathes and other machine tools were covered in dust. I could understand any workforce apprehension, as one had to wonder if London Transport at this time really needed both Chiswick and the Aldenham establishment. As requested, I wrote a report as to my findings, but was never told what effect, if any, the contents came to have on the end result – namely the closure of Aldenham.

As I mentioned above, we were now firmly in the age of the Business Plan and the need for the new undertakings to ensure that theirs would be sufficiently well based – and showing a satisfactory forecast to enable it to be signed off by the Ministers. The obvious conclusion to be reached here was – no suitable Business Plan – equals no ongoing transport undertaking, but then realisation dawned. Deregulation Sunday was not going to be a day of undue concern, for even in 1986 Sunday traffic was not of over-great moment, but Monday morning was going to be a different matter altogether.

There could be a situation, early in the morning, when passengers were standing waiting at stops, there were buses stood in their garage, and men all ready to take them out on the road, but all would be at a standstill as no relevant Business Plan had been signed off. Such a situation would have been intolerable and so precautions had to be taken. These took two forms. Firstly, ensure that every Business Plan that came to be presented had been compiled with as much attention to detail as was practical, and secondly do what was possible to ensure no new company would come to fail within two years from deregulation. I drew up a list of all the municipal concerns, ranking them in four categories.

Division one: Those which obviously had a clear future before them.

Division two: Those that should succeed after some minor tweaking.

Division three: Those that could be on the margin.

Division four: Those either too small to have a long-term future, or which were at this time in the apparent doldrums.

It made interesting reading and in the event I was not far wrong with my assessments. Consequently, I began to travel some more, taking in mainly division three and four concerns, and here, though I knew it not at the time, was the job that I would take up after my time at Marsham Street had come to an end.

I went on a Welsh safari by car, when my way home led me close to Aberdare where I called in at the Transport Offices to pay a short courtesy call, to find that the General Manager had gone off sick and seemed unlikely to be able to return to duty. His deputy, who was holding the fort, was very concerned about his and the company's future, so would I please discuss these weighty matters with him in detail. I replied that I simply had not time to do so that day as I was scheduled to make another call elsewhere later on, but would ring him when I was back in Marsham Street the following week, and then make the necessary appointment with him.

To my shame I completely forgot that promise until a full two weeks had passed. Then I did ring the Aberdare office, to receive a totally unexpected response. The young lady on the switchboard told me that she had been instructed when I did phone to put me through, not to the Deputy, but to the Council's Chief Executive who promptly came on the line. He then told me that the Deputy had also left on sick leave, placing the Council and its Transport Department in an impossible situation, so would I please come to Aberdare as soon as possible and there meet the Council members to go over the situation with them. This I agreed to do and the proposed meeting duly took place on the 30th July. I was asked how it was possible to recover from the ongoing situation, and without any pre-thought I said, "Easy, you need to recruit someone like me, a retired transport manager. Plenty of my former colleagues are in the process of taking early retirement and I can provide you with some possible and suitable names here and now".

When I had finished speaking one Councillor said, "Why can't you do the necessary?" My reply was to the effect that I could not see how it might be possible, employed as I was by the Department of Transport. However, after some more persuasion, I promised that at the least I would go and fork the ground over, and do what I reasonably could to ensure Cynon Valley Transport, as it was known, would come to occupy a place in the post-deregulation sun.

So I started a slow but sure shift in my activities. I spent less time in Marsham Street as we approached the finality of deregulation and ever more in Cynon Valley. I still had some work to do for the Department though, until my service there came to an end and I received a letter from Mr David Mitchell MP thanking me for the work that I had done during my time with the Bill team.

Here it is only right and proper that I express my appreciation to Mr AP Brown, the then Under Secretary in charge of bus policy. I would also like to express my appreciation to his principal lieutenants: assistant secretaries Gillian Ashmore, Peter Pickering and Harry Fawcett; and all the other members of the team for the way in which they accepted me, outsider though I was, during the time when I was having a daily association with them.

Once the Bill had become law and the Passenger Transport Industry had settled down to meet the challenge provided by deregulation, and all things appertaining thereto, the Civil Servants that I had come to know went off to work in other government fields. Under Secretary Patrick Brown became involved in the privatisation of the water industry, and continued with this and other activities as he rose through the ranks of the Civil Service. He was later appointed Permanent Under Secretary of State there, and so became the head of the Department of Transport, where he was awarded a knighthood in the honours list. Now, as Sir Patrick Brown, he continues his interest in the Industry, currently being Chairman of the Go Ahead Group and its subsidiary companies.

During the period when I was making my visits around the country, this Ipswich Bristol RE with ECW body, a combination I was familiar with at Leicester, was typical of the vehicles in service with their fleet at the time. When I allocated the municipal operators to their respective 'Divisions', who could have known precisely which were to be the eleven survivors, or that Ipswich would be one of them..

Cynon Valley Transport purchased a Bristol RELL single-decker which was overhauled and repainted by Southend Transport, the original owner, before being delivered to Aberdare. It is shown in the Southend works yard prior to delivery.

Cynon Valley Transport's Ford midibus also received the Southend treatment. Here it is awaiting despatch to Aberdare.

2 – A Welsh Interlude

Realising that Cynon Valley Transport had been verging on the point of disaster, the Council members obviously wanted to give their new transport limited company as good a start in life as possible, and so sanctioned some useful expenditure. A substantial metal fence was erected around the depot, which certainly improved security, and in so doing thwarted a local farmer who, with the old adage, 'the shortest distance between two points is a straight line', firmly in mind used to drive his flock of sheep through the place, as I was told had been the case in the past.

Now, before I came to have a local professional association, I had made just one previous visit to Aberdare. Geoffrey Harding had been my predecessor as Head of Engineering at Halifax but left to become Deputy General Manager at Rochdale. He then applied for and obtained the Managership of the then Aberdare undertaking, when over the years we had become good friends. As a result, during the 1958 weekend when I was in transit from Halifax to Plymouth to take up my Deputy General Manager's post in that city, I made a detour via Aberdare, staying with Geoffrey when he showed me round the undertaking. The depot and office facilities as they then existed were primitive to say the least, but Geoffrey could be very persuasive, and so had managed to introduce new buses into the fleet, and also to have the Council agree to the building of new and enlarged premises on the Gadlys site. Fleet strength at that time was 43, with 16 double-deckers of AEC, Bristol and Guy manufacture, with single-deck buses from the same firms making up the balance. Some of these were fitted with wooden seating which reflected the large number of miners that came to be carried, it being said that there were once 16 coal mines local to the area of the Urban District Council.

I now had to become much more familiar with the territory, the bus fleet and routes and all associated therewith, and so I came to discover that the undertaking had had a very interesting history. The Council had come to the conclusion, back in the October of 1901, that it should seek powers to allow the construction of a tramway system, when at the same time the Mountain Ash authority was seeking to do likewise. The intention was that the tracks should be joined at Abercwmboi, which when added to Aberdare's 4½ mile intention would give a continuous route of 9⅓ miles along the floor of the valley. Alas, things did not go according to plan and Mountain Ash never did possess a working tramway, whilst the Aberdare Council had to contend with a good deal of opposition, much of this coming from the local railway companies. Eventually, at the third attempt, Aberdare was successful in obtaining tramway powers, but it also gained authority to build six trolleybus routes as feeder to the tramways; this was the first such combined operation in the country. The contracts to build the tramways were let in February 1912, the system being opened at long last on the 9th October 1913.

The backbone was the 2½ mile long 3ft 6in gauge single track with loop lines, a tramway that ran from the Old Cemetery at Trecynon through the town centre to Clarence Street, Aberaman, together with a short branch at Gadlys, which led to the new four bay tramway shed. This had two extra bays to house the eight trolleybuses also taken into stock, for working the four routes that were actually built. At the Old Cemetery, on the far side of the Great Western railways level crossing, was the terminus for the trolleybus service that ran up the valley side to Cwmdare which opened on the 16th of February 1914, but this was not as long as the powers allowed. At the southern Clarence Street end were the termini of two more trolleybus services, to Cwmaman and Capcoch, which were opened simultaneously on the 2nd February 1914. Finally, a town centre to Abernant route was opened a little before the others on the 15th January. At first sight there seemed little point in constructing this route as Abernant was not actually a densely populated area. However, it did have the inevitable coal mine and a railway station, trains leaving for Merthyr via a tunnel under the local mountain or to Hirwaun in the opposite direction. Both the Abernant and Cwmaman routes had a steep gradient as the vehicles all-too-soon discovered.

Sadly, the Town Council had invested in the Cedes Stoll overhead line and vehicle systems, and the front wheel driving motors began to suffer all-too-many armature failures. Bigger motors were then supplied, but made little difference, whilst the atrocious condition of the local roads also gave rise to excessive wear and tear. So bad was that to Capcoch that the service was withdrawn on the 16th February 1916, never to be resumed, but the other three staggered on through the period of the Great War when reliability was ever-suspect and spare parts almost unobtainable.

The Council soon became very aware of all the attendant shortcomings, and so in 1915 they obtained powers to build two tramway extensions and to run motor buses. Nevertheless, those tramway extensions were yet again a long time coming. At the same time they tried to build a reserved sleeper-tracked tramway from the Old Cemetery to Hirwaun, but again railway opposition put paid to that scheme. The extension from Clarence Street to Abercwmboi was opened on the 24th February 1922, and that on a new series of roads to Cwmaman on the 8th November 1922.

To work these extensions, twelve new double-deck open-topped trams were obtained from the Brush Company that had built all the tramway rolling stock, so the Council now had 26 cars; the ten original single-deckers, the four 1914 additions, and the latest batch of twelve. Much of the track from town to Clarence Street was also doubled. The trolleybus fleet was down to five, four in working order, with only the Abernant service continuing to be operated. The Cwmaman service had been withdrawn in February 1919, the Cwmdare route closing in 1922. By this time the Council had begun to employ its bus operating powers, owning seven Tilling-Stevens single-deckers.

Having digested the above facts I began to look into the current position, to find that Cynon Valley Transport had 36 vehicles:
19 Leyland Mark 1 Nationals;
10 Leyland-engined Bristol RE's;
1 Dodge midibus;
6 Ford mini buses.
Five of the latter were recent acquisitions.

The double-deckers and all the other buses in use in Geoffrey Harding's day had long gone, as had wooden seats as there was now not a single working colliery in the district – neither were there any passenger train services.

Southend also repaired and retrimmed some of Cynon Valley Transport's Leyland Nationals, as shown in this interior view. The exterior was also repainted into Cynon Valley Transport's green and white livery.

The former town centre Taff Vale station with its Pontypridd and Cardiff services had been totally demolished and a new road covered a good deal of the track bed. The ruin of the former Great Western establishment was still visible and track was laid through the site. This track was carrying trains working to or from the Tower Colliery, which was located beyond Hirwaun.

Almost my first action was to strengthen operating supervision, bringing the Inspectorate up to four and making a surprise appointment with a Chief Inspector, and here I could not have made a better choice. In the meantime, the Council had given me the tenancy of a fairly new flat and had nominated three members of the Council to sit on the Company Board, which, with the Commercial Director, a local man with previous service, and myself, made up a total of five Directors. I must here pay tribute to my Council-sponsored Board colleagues who at all times were as helpful and supportive as they could be, and who agreed that all disciplinary matters would be left in my hands with no appeals coming before the Board, which was quite a change from previous practice. Geoff Harding told me that he could not dismiss anyone unless the case was placed before the full Council, which had to pass a minute agreeing to his intention, when they could then be implemented. I thought back to Leicester… Another staff change occurred right at the beginning when the Company's Engineer elected to seek retirement on health grounds, but fortunately his number two was able to stand in very effectively. This was just as well, for, as was the case in Leicester, the undertaking maintained all the Council's wheeled transport, and, as was to be expected, putting right defective refuse collection units formed a major part of the work.

Living history, July 1987. At the exhibition the author meets Joe Bruton, then aged 92, and in truly remarkable health. Joe joined Aberdare Tramways on 22nd January 1914 as a trolleybus conductor and retiring in 1958 as an Inspector. How I wished that I had had a tape-recorder with me, but sadly his fascinating accounts of bygone transport days are lost for ever.

Cynon Valley Transport mounted a small exhibition in Aberdare's main street to publicise its improved services and new livery. Fortunately, the weather was good so plenty of people stopped and looked it over, many buying a timetable.

A Bob Davies Cynon Valley Transport 1987 timetable booklet produced to publicise the introduction of the 20 minute frequencies, and a Charlie's cars minibus travel guide valid from 19th October 1988.

Unfortunately, the traffic side was not as well organised as it should have been, service registrations only being deposited towards the last minute, but fortunately the long-service and now-retired Traffic Superintendent, Mr Byron Newman, agreed to return to work and draft out new schedules.

We were also light on timetables and general publicity material, so another retired ex-colleague, Bob Davies of Doncaster and West Yorkshire PTE fame, was brought in to do all that was needed here. Financially it was all very marginal, but if no additional competition came over the hill we should be able to keep the head of the Company above water, and perhaps introduce various improvements.

First things first though, and problem number one was service frequencies.

The main bus route, as was only to be expected, was based on the line of the former tramway services, the vehicles running from Abercwmboi through the town to the Old Cemetery, and then continuing to Hirwaun, deviating off the main road to serve the large council estate at Penywaun. This only ran on a half-hourly headway, which was just inviting competition to enter the picture, and enter it did in December when the Clayton Jones organisation began to run over the full length of the route, starting though from Pontypridd and taking in Abercynon and Mountain Ash in the process. That 30 minute frequency should never have been allowed to continue, but I simply had neither the time nor the local knowledge to improve the situation.

Needless to say the National Welsh ex-NBC concern, now privatised and led by Mr Brian Noton, was firmly ensconced in the Aberdare area too, and was not going to let CVT cream off some of its passengers without a struggle. We had a surplus of Ford-based minibuses, and another problem was to find some suitable work for them in addition to their existing use on lightly-loaded services, and certain evening workings. A brand new set of services thus came into being.

A bus started its run by leaving the Gadlys depot which helped in making staff and vehicle changeovers, although depot workings were licensed to carry passengers. It then entered the town centre to go to Cwmbach, then covering the upper part of the Brodeg Estate by serving Brynhir. The service then ran across the valley to Capcoch, before passing through Abercwmboi to gain Mountain Ash. The buses then ran through the centre, to change direction by running round the one-way streets at Mount Pleasant. They then left Mountain Ash for the hillside village of Cefnpennar, to return to Mountain Ash and the Mount Pleasant circuit for the second time. They now left Mountain Ash for the Newtown area, before going back to Mountain Ash and traversing the circle for the third time prior to leaving via the outward route to Aberdare and Gadlys once more. The round trip fitted nicely into a two hour running time, so two buses could provide an hourly frequency.

At the Aberdare end the minibuses were, in part, superimposed on the main Brodeg circulars with their extension to Rose Row. This was another major route worked by big buses and again only a half hourly frequency was provided, as was the case on another important route to Glynhafod, which was an extension of the post war tramway service to Cwmaman. This was steeply graded, and had more than its fair share of sharp corners which had given rise to difficulties in tramway days.

Continuing with the theme. After having a Trojan and a Morris minibus Aberdare Transport acquired this solitary Ford A series example. It is shown in the Gadlys depot yard in Cynon Valley Transport's orange, green and cream colours with that new security fence much in evidence. I asked former GM, Derek Hyde, "why buy a midibus?" His answer was "to serve an old-peoples/disabled home." A social but quite uneconomic facility.

An unusual Aberdare vehicle of earlier years was this Morris minibus, then fleet number 9.

It was not legally possible to change the initial service registrations for some time, but the 'close season' came to an end, and CVT was then ready to make some improvements. Without any extra rolling stock, and without taking on any extra staff, it was possible to introduce 20 minute frequencies on all the major routes with effect from Sunday 1st February 1987, but to do this schedules had to be tightened up. Needless to say this gave rise to some heartburn amongst the traffic staff, and talk of a strike came to be aired. Here some firm talking was necessary and the position of the company was made plain to the staff. Thanks to the competition being experienced, the financial situation was very marginal, and it was possible that if the services were stopped, then there was no certainty that they would or could start again. The staff members, to their credit, took heed of the message, and no strike came to materialise. Even without any extra bodies on the books, extra man hours would be involved, plus the additional fuel costs – and more mileage meant more repair work, and who could say with certainty that there would be sufficient income forthcoming to cover these additional costs?

One other part of the business was also increasing. As part of its initial support the Council agreed to fund the purchase of three dual-purpose semi-coaches. These were based on Leyland Tiger chassis with 218 horsepower engines and semi-automatic gearboxes; two had Duple bodies, the other was by Plaxton. They were second-hand but in very good condition, and proved to be very acceptable.

Not quite so good were some of the Nationals, so the worst ones were slowly but surely rehabilitated and often re-trimmed. At the same time the Board agreed with my suggestion that a CVT vehicle should be instantly recognisable, and as one of our competitors vehicles were painted red, CVT's began to appear in an orange, green and cream livery that was not unknown elsewhere, although the shade of green adopted was not the same as the one applied in the Halifax area of old. Things now settled down for a wee while, and the number of passengers being carried did tend to increase.

The new services included an extension from Abercwmboi to the large Fernhill Estate that lay off the main Cardiff /Mountain Ash Road on the western hillside that had never previously enjoyed a bus service, but we did not have it to ourselves, as National Welsh also started a competitive service to the estate. It was, though, quite worthwhile. A few minor improvements to other existing routes were made on the 1st February, but there was one brand new possibility that I carefully considered.

As I mentioned in the early part of this chapter, the Mountain Ash Urban District Council had had aspirations to construct a tramway from its northern boundary at Abercwmboi, to its southern one at Abercynon, where hopefully the Aberdare UDC would take its rails to the aforementioned boundary. In the event Mountain Ash never did have its tramway which obviously would have been built to the 3ft 6in gauge, whilst the Abedare rails stopped at Clarence Street with the short-lived trolleybus route from Clarence Street to Capcoch. At last, after the end of the First World War, the tramway was extended to Abercwmboi which served the needs of residents living along the floor of the valley. The trams came, and went in April 1935 when buses took over, but never entered Mountain Ash, which came to be served by numerous independents.

Stranger in the camp. After my departure, Leicester City transport wished to sell the Dennis Falcon/Duple single-deckers. Cynon Valley Transport borrowed No.93 for trials and it is seen here in Aberdare. Unfortunately, the price was too high and so it was regretfully returned with thanks.

Once you left the valley floor steep gradients are encountered. Here Aberdare AEC Reliance, No.4, comes up the hillside from Clarence Street. No wonder those early trolleybuses had trouble negotiating routes with such characteristics. They would not do AEC 470 power units much good either, with their wet cylinder liners and head gaskets which were prone to failure.

Thanks to the later passing of the Local Government Re-organisation Act, Aberdare and Mountain Ash were amalgamated to form the new Cynon Valley District Council. As a result the new District came to possess a piece of territory that was almost detached from the main land area and was known as Ynsybwl. I reasoned that the Council would be quite pleased to see the district provided with a through bus service to Aberdare, and so we went on several prospecting expeditions.

The suggested route would run down the old tramway line to Abercwmboi, and then follow our February 1987 extension to the entrance to the Fernhill Estate. From there, it would continue to Mountain Ash and thence to Abercynon, when it would branch off to the right to run along the base of the hills to Carnetown. There were, of course, the usual snags. To run an hourly service would need two mini buses for starters, and only one could be made readily available. Then there was a very narrow piece of highway between Abercynon and Carnetown that would almost certainly give rise to clearance difficulties, and finally came the big question 'Would it pay?' Going down the Valley to Abercynon could well cause heartburn in the breasts of our competitors, and might have resulted in more counter activities in and around Aberdare, where we already had quite sufficient.

There was an alternative, and that was to take the bull by the horns, run into Pontypridd and then out again to Carnetown and the Glyncoch Estate, but that meant running over one of Taff Ely's two really profitable routes. I doubted if there was sufficient income in the pot to provide the two of us with a living, even if we had sufficient big buses to provide a decent time table with at the very least a thirty minute frequency. In the end I came to the conclusion that a wait-and-see policy should be adopted, when, if we were able to improve the financial situation and obtain two more vehicles – either full size or mini depending on the route to be adopted, ie direct from Abercvnon, or down the length of the valley and via Pontypridd – we might be able to start to experiment. However, as it happened I was never in Aberdare long enough to find out.

I then turned my attention to the offices. Although the whole building was of quite recent construction, it was not well-endowed with office space, and more accommodation was wanted. There was, though, a very easy solution. To the right of the main entrance was a metal grating, through which, in earlier days, coke had been tipped into the fuel store, but now the boilers were gas-fired and so the area was disused. A door was driven from the entrance foyer to the store, and this was then given a wooden floor. It was quite a sizeable area, so when the walls had been plastered and decorated, and the ceiling suitably improved, it provided a most convenient office for the Traffic Superintendent and the Chief Inspector.

Their traffic department was much busier than it had been and we had introduced a somewhat marginal ploy. A bus coming from Fernhill and Abercwmboi arrived in the main Hiwaun stop in Cardiff Street Aberdare, and when the passengers for the town centre had alighted, those travelling onwards with the driver moved to a bus that was also standing at the stop. This had been acting as a mobile waiting room when passengers going north could enter and take a seat. The driver (omo) took the fares, and then the vehicle left for the trip to Hirwaun. The vehicle from the southern end of the route then took its place, and so we managed to bag the lion's share of town centre passengers who might otherwise have boarded a competing vehicle.

One of Cynon Valley Transport's nineteen Leyland Nationals, No.25, stands in the Gadlys depot yard in its traditional maroon and white livery.

In new territory. Cynon Valley Transport Bristol, No.13, has arrived at the Fernhill Estate terminal loop and will soon be ready to return to Aberdare and Hirwaun on that new 'main line' 20 minute frequency. A competing National Wales vehicle prepares to do likewise.

We then settled down to review the vehicles and staff that were available and came to the conclusion that with a modicum of adjustment we could lift those 20 minute main-line frequencies to ones of 15 minutes. The necessary applications were deposited with the Traffic Commissioners, and the better services were introduced. Then came an unexpected development. The fortnightly Notices and Proceedings announced that CVT was going to be called in for Public Inquiry to explain why it had been running unregistered journeys, those words being reinforced by a letter addressed to me from the Traffic Commissioner's office. Consequently, I rang that establishment and asked to speak to the clerk to the Commissioners, who for this purpose we will call John, although that was not his real name. The conversation then went like this:

Me: "What's all this nonsense about a public inquiry, are you certain?"

John: "It's no good Geoffrey, you are not as white as you like to make out. We have been monitoring your services and they are nothing like the registrations that we have here".

Me: "I know you had monitors on". I told him the date, and that they were in situ at four places, and I told him the times adding. "We knew they were there within ten minutes of their starting. You really ought to equip them with less visible attire".

John: "Well, we have all the evidence. Mr Jackson has seen it and wants you before him when you will have to answer some awkward questions".

Me: "I do not think so".

John: "Sanctions could well be applied".

Me: "Two questions. When we want to vary our registrations, have we not to fill in the appropriate forms, give you 42-day's-notice, and send you a cheque to cover the requisite fee?"

John: "You know very well that those things are necessary".

Me: "Well John, we improved our service frequency from every 20 minutes to every 15 minutes. We gave you the 42-day notice, sending you the forms and of course the cheque. And by the way do not say you never received them as I have our bank statement before me and you have drawn the fee as is shown thereon. You have been monitoring our workings on registrations that no longer applied. How about an apology and confirmation that there is not going to be a hearing?".

John: "I will ring you back later".

He did – that afternoon – and he was a very chastened Civil Servant, but we never did get an apology.

On the engineering side, more buses were repainted and put into better order, but it was not yet possible to think positively about placing any orders for some new ones. It was, though, possible to persuade the Cleansing Department to try a refuse collection vehicle with automatic transmission and hydraulic packing equipment. Such machines were, according to our Dennis friends, far more reliable and long-lasting, so much so that the UK market for new machines shrank from 1,800 a year to around 800/900 vehicles.

When I started work in Aberdare, I was 61 years old and in pretty good health, so there seemed to be no reason, barring accidents, that I should not keep continuing in employment until I reached 65 in about three and

Cynon Valley Transport minibus, No.5 (C604 KVP), is a Freight Rover Sherpa with 16-seat Carlyle bodywork. It sports the new orange, green and cream livery, and is seen in the depot yard. Note the new security fence which can be seen behind the vehicle.

Far from home. I was invited to a Yorkshire Rider commemoration event, so for old time's sake I took Cynon Valley Transport's Plaxton-bodied Tiger with me and our Chief Inspector, who returned the vehicle to its base. Here it is parked in an open area of Skircoat Road depot.

a half years time. My wife shared the same view, and had ensured that my very acceptable rented two bedroomed modern flat was furnished to a very comfortable standard. Nevertheless my stay in the town turned out to be of fairly short duration.

Change began one afternoon when I was sat at my desk and the phone rang. The CVT switchboard operator said that a Mr Hawker wanted to speak to me, but as I knew no one of that name, I did wonder why. On the basis though that you speak to any first-time caller at least once as you cannot be aware of why they wished to contact you, and they just might be worthwhile, I asked our young lady to put him through.

He started of by saying he was in a quandary. He wanted to speak to the Mr Hilditch who had been with the Department of Transport, but there were two people in the reference books of that name, so if I was not that person, would I accept his immediate apologies for the intrusion. I indicated that I was indeed the man that he sought; the other being my son who was then Engineering Director with the Southend Municipal Transport Company. Mr Hawker then asked had I a service contract with CVT; I told him if I had, or had not, it was no business of his. He continued though, saying he hoped that my answer would have been in the negative as he was approaching me on behalf of a Mr PR McEnhill, who had a proposition to put to me, and who in consequence would be obliged if I would meet up with him in his Salisbury Office where all would be revealed.

I was rather dubious as I had not heard ever of Mr PR McEnhill, so I suggested that if the gentleman really did want to put a proposition to me it was a pity that he had not phoned me direct, instead of making an approach via an intermediary, and perhaps Mr Hawker would be so kind as to convey those sentiments to him. He said he would and I put the phone down. A day or two later I received a call from the elusive one, and he then told me something about himself, but added that he could and would tell me the whole story if I would accept his invitation to meet up with him in his Endless Street office. In the end I said that I would and we fixed on a date and time about a week ahead.

On the day, I paid my first real visit to Salisbury, having previously passed through on the train and had also changed buses at the bus station which I found flanked Endless Street, only it was far from having an affinity with its name being surprisingly short. The Endless offices were located in an old but quite large town house, and Mr McEnhill also was worthy of the same description as he was physically very well built. He saw me almost as soon as I had arrived, and went on to tell me that he ran a small group of units, two principal facets of the business being the production of equipment that reduced central heating plants of industrial proportions putting the source of Legionnaires disease into the atmosphere. They also provided the homes for people with acute respiratory disease with oxygen systems that were fitted into every room the sufferer used, where an oxygen mask could be easily plugged in. This though was just incidental.

He had wanted to buy, and had bid for some of the ex-NBC engineering businesses that had been put on the market of late, but had lost out through a competitor putting in higher bids. This, though, had wetted his appetite, and

West Yorkshire Olympian 5006 had been put into the old Halifax colours. I borrowed it and we ran it in service on the main Fernhill-Abercwmboi-Aberdare-Hirwaun route. On this journey the main road is traffic-free.

The Cynon Valley Transport Plaxton-bodied Leyland Tiger dual-purpose coach, in Halifax style livery, stands in Aberdare.

now he wanted to try to secure some of the operating companies that were coming up for sale. He had substantial backing from an American Bank now available, but he needed a transport professional to join him in setting up a worthwhile group. This person would in effect be Group Managing Director. He had with him another Director, Mr Stanley McCardle, where together they set the scene and outlined the sort of remuneration package that I could expect. What did I say?

Well, as things stood at that moment, this was all rather pie-in-the-sky. There was nothing concrete, only desires, and I did not know all that I felt was necessary, so I must approach what on its face was an interesting proposition with caution. I would not join them in the short term, but would provide some assistance on a part time basis, where I would try to fit in any Endless Holding's requirements.

So we ended our conversations, and I made my way home to Torbay.

At this time the rule was that any person or group could bid for, and if the offers were the best, acquire three – but not more than three – major ex-NBC operating companies. They could also buy a single minor unit, sales being handled by the Sales Team that was being set up in my time at the Department under a Mr Rodney Lumb, who was backed by several Sales Negotiators. They would be present when a prospective buyer paid a visit to his target to indulge in the process known as Due Diligence, to give him some idea of the worth of the concern, and the size of the bid that was felt to be attractive to the seller without being over extravagant. From this time on I gradually became more and more involved with Endless possible purchase activities, and going from time-to-time to visit concerns that could be attractive purchases and looking them over, before Ray McEnhill worked up a bid, something at which he was very good indeed.

I told my Aberdare Council Member Board colleagues about the new opportunity that had come my way, and so I found myself at the Board meeting when I indicated that I should now be tendering my resignation. I told them of the salary I had been offered and I was then asked if I would stay on for an identical package, but this I had to decline on the grounds of the company not being able to afford the figure involved. Also that I could not accept such an increase when I had been responsible for making life more hectic and not just as lucrative for the company staff. I was then asked if I would help select a successor, and also stay on as a Board member, and as I had been treated so well by the Cynon Valley Authority I replied that I would be delighted to do so.

My successor came to be Norman Kay, the then recently-retired Director General of the South Yorkshire PTE, and one could think that after such a high profile job nobody could settle down to running a small concern like Cynon Valley Transport, but there were no grounds for any such fears.

As a teenager Norman had obtained a situation with the former Ramsbottom Municipal Transport Undertaking, a concern which also had invested in an early trolleybus system but wisely chose an installation that was much more reliable than that of Cedes-Stoll design and manufacture.

At the time Norman took up his post, Sidney Parsons was the General Manager, a position he held from 1920 to 1952, and he very soon began to employ his new recruit as a veritable 'Jack of all trades'. Consequently, there was nothing that

Norman did not know about the operation of small bus undertakings, and so he took over the tenancy of my furnished flat and with his wife Eileen, he soon settled down to life in Aberdare, where I had no doubt that he would take the business on.

I left with a little pleasure thinking that thanks to my arrival a municipal company was enabled to survive, but there was one thing I did not miss, this being my twice weekly trips over the old River Severn suspension bridge. All the time I was travelling to and from Aberdare it was under repair, having the floor relaaid, so there was normally only one lane of traffic opened, and as the new bridge had not then been constructed it was heavily trafficked. Crossing on a windy day was not pleasant, and of course if that wind became strong then the structure would be closed, which meant I had to make a tedious journey via Gloucester, when on one occasion I was nearly written off. An artic came down a hill fast, got into a skid, and the trailer turned through 90° and was sweeping my side of the road like a Boadicea chariot, but then it began to go back into line on its own side of the highway, missing my car with very little to spare.

I finally continued as a Board Member until Norman elected to retire in 1989, and resigned when George Shaw took over in turn as he was a stranger to me, and obviously wanted to have some of his trusted old colleagues helping him in the CVT work.

I cannot though, leave the Cynon Valley without making a mention of a possible might-have-been.

On the 7th December 1985, Commercial Motor published its annual review of the fleets of Britain's major bus operators. It recorded a fleet total of 31 for Cynon Valley Transport, which was one vehicle less in stock than the previous year. This drop, though, pales into insignificance when compared to the statistics shown against the name of the National Welsh Company. In 1974, this organisation had a fleet strength of 550 vehicles, but, in the issue dated as above, that total was down by 150 to just 400, with 6 Leyland Tigers and 21 Ford Transits on order. With a cut like that the financial situation cannot have been very good, but no signs of weakness showed in the way the Company competed with CVT and with the Clayton Jones concern in my day.

Not too long after Norman Kay and I left Aberdare, National Welsh did collapse, when I believe the Directors of CVT mounted a bid for National Welsh's former Aberdare area services. There would seem to have been an ideal chance here to amalgamate both sets of operations into a much stronger whole which could well have survived, but such was not the case. I do not know just what did come to transpire, but in the end both undertakings faded from the scene, and the site of the former CVT Gadlys depot is now covered by a supermarket.

So another municipal bus company came to perish, a type of unit that now borders on the extinct, with only 11 still existing in 2013.

Shamrock and Rambler's Charlie's cars minibuses were finished in green and white, so I had these colours applied to the coach fleet as shown in this photograph of a Plaxton-bodied Leyland Tiger.

A Shamrock and Rambler coach in its pre-Drawlane livery prepares to work the very first 'Town Tracker' service departure from Weymouth at 9.30am on the 19th October 1987. Buses left every two hours for Dorchester, Bournemouth and Southampton.

3 – In the big time

The first Endless acquisition turned out to be the Shamrock and Rambler concern based in Yeomans Way, Bournemouth. From 1929 Shamrock and Rambler had a variety of owners until June 1966, when United Transport Services sold it to the Transport Holding Company, who then placed it under the control of Hants and Dorset. Shamrock and Rambler was formed after the amalgamation on the 8th April 1924 of the two concerns that figured in its name, when at a later stage in June 1963, another Bournemouth coach concern, Charlie's Cars, was purchased, this then had eleven vehicles. Charlie's Cars had been owned by a Mr Charles Pound who was obviously fond of Albion-based coaches, and it was in one of these with a Harrington body that my then fiancé and I left Manchester for a touring holiday based in Bournemouth. Our Albion was pedestrian in the extreme, but it did take us sagely, even if rather slowly, to our Bournemouth hotel.

It then must have fallen sick because for the rest of our stay to the next weekend it was replaced by an almost new Tilling-Stevens luxury coach. That marque had been in slow decline in pre-war days from about 1932/3, but prior to that thanks to its Tilling connection, a goodly number of Tilling-Stevens buses were to be seen on British Roads. My local bus company North Western Road Car Company had a very large fleet of them, buying just over 400 between 1924 and 1931. Tilling-Stevens had tried to return to the big time by buying the Southport firm of Vulcan and transferring production to its Maidstone works, and then producing two revolutionary chassis. These were the 'Successor' passenger chassis, and the 'Yeoman' intended for goods work. They had flat horizontal engines then known as 'pancakes', independent suspension and various other new features. In fact, it was all so new that no one was tempted to chance buying one which was certainly

A typical rebuilt Tilling-Stevens with luxurious seating, the body being constructed by Eastern Counties of Lowestoft. These were daily performers on the Oldham and Saddleworth area routes.

Bournemouth Square is the location of this night view of ECW-bodied Bristol VRT which will depart for Poole. Wilts and Dorset was a major competitor for Bournemouth's Yellow Buses following deregulation.

The Triangle was used by Bournemouth for storing vehicles between the peak hours. A Wilts and Dorset Leyland Olympian in the express livery is on the long run to Salisbury.

a shame. After the war Tilling-Stevens produced its heavyweight passenger chassis with either Gardner or Meadows engines, and it was one of the latter varieties that powered our temporary conveyance. It has to be said that the Meadows engine was not noted for having a long life but with 10.3-litres it could outperform most of the opposition, and sweeping quite quietly through the Dorset country side on a gorgeous day, with the sun roof back and the radio playing Mantovani-style music showed us just what luxury coach travel should be like. A TS.K6MA9 chassis with Meadows engine cost £2,310 or £4,365 with 33-seat Outfield coach body.

We returned home on the Saturday in the Albion that must have recovered from its indisposition, and I regret to say that I truly wished it had not. The sight of a post-war Tilling-Stevens today is a very rare one, as around 1950 it was bought by the Rootes Group that ended production at Maidstone, together with those vehicles badged as Vulcan. These in the main were for goods use and had seemed quite popular, but to leave us all guessing, for the Maidstone plant turned over to making the TS-3 engine, but did the initials TS mean Tilling-Stevens or Two Stroke? I for one have never known the answer.

But to return to Shamrock and Rambler. In 1985 the concern, split from Hants and Dorset control, had 43 vehicles. There was a solitary Leyland PD3 and a solitary Bristol, only this was not what it seemed. A Bristol MW had been involved in an accident so it was stripped down to the underframe, and onto that was built a replica charabanc body. The ensemble certainly was very eye catching. There were also 28 Leyland Leopard coaches, two Bovas used mainly to carry the musicians of the Bournemouth Symphony Orchestra, and eleven MCW Metroliners with another three then being on order.

It had been run from the combined coach station and depot in Holderness Road, but by the time Endless – soon to be renamed the Drawlane Transport Group PLC – took over, changes had been made. A new depot had been built on the edge of the town at Yeomans Way, this being close to the also brand new Hampshire Shopping Centre, and this gave Shamrock and Rambler a third string to its bow. The first string consisted of doing what the concern had always done, namely running private hire, excursion and either long or short tours which employed the coaches.

The second string utilised the now 14-strong fleet of Metroliners, and three of these finished to a more luxurious standard with wider seat spacing were used on the Bournemouth to London Rapide service. The other eleven worked the standard National Express type of interurban service, which again connected the Bournemouth area with London.

The third string was responsible for the acquisition of a number of minibuses painted green and cream and adorned with the 'Charlie's Cars' legend that had previously fallen out of use. A range of mini bus services were now provided from parts of Bournemouth and Poole to the Hampshire Centre; as quite a recent innovation traffic levels had still to be built up.

The National Express workings formed a major part of the business but here one had to take care. The National Express supervisory staff on duty at the London Victoria Coach Station were very keen, and if a concern did not meet their standards then penalties ensued. Run a vehicle on a timetabled working

Ready for the fray. Metroliners in their National Express colours. No.3121 in the foreground was new in 1984 and had a 57/23-seat body. It was one of the vehicles shown here which were received by Shamrock and Rambler that year; they were numbered from 3112-21.

The third string. Charlie's Cars Ford minibuses are standing in the bus station of the new Hampshire Centre. 201-9, of 1986, had Carlyle 16-seat bodies, as had 230-5 of 1987. Nos.210-29, also of 1987, had FreightRover Sherpa chassis and Dormobile bodies. The six ex-Yorkshire Rider 16-seaters had Freight Rover Sherpa chassis and Optare bodies, and were numbered Charlie 705 to Charlie 710. These were acquired in October 1987.

Charlie's Cars competed with Bournemouth Transport, as seen in this view taken in the town centre. Freight Rover/Dormobile, No.228, is on the move whilst one of Bournemouth's many Alexander-bodied Daimler Fleetlines is picking up passengers.

Not what it seems. Shamrock and Rambler owned this apparent vintage vehicle, only it wasn't! It was based on a modern Bristol LH chassis and it certainly attracted a lot of attention. It was licensed to carry passengers.

Signing up. The purchase of Midland Red North by Drawlane Ltd is signed and sealed at the National Bus Company's head office. From the left are Rear Admiral Stanley McArdle, director of Drawlane; Christopher Campbell, executive board member of NBC; and Geoffrey Hilditch, managing director of Drawlane.

Shamrock and Rambler's Metroliners were leased for use on the National Express contracts which expired before the vehicle lease. National Express set up a puppet company to run the London services, leaving Shamrock and Rambler with 13 redundant Metroliners which were then allocated to other group companies. Here, one of three sent to Midland Red North, has been repainted and stands at Tamworth prior to working an express service to Birmingham. Once the leases on the vehicles came to an end, prompt disposal followed.

that was not in NBC livery, (unless it was a necessary duplicate), or fail to show proper destination blinds, or run undesirably late, all gave rise to deductions being made from the particular payment involved. Worse was not to run at all, or suffer a breakdown en route, and here the Metroliners were just not as reliable as one would have hoped. They did, though, cover a very considerable mileage. For example, one track involved running light to Poole, and then heading for London via Bournemouth and Southampton. On arrival in the capital a return trip was made to and from Southampton to be followed by a second such return working. Finally, the Metroliner was scheduled to head for Bournemouth and Poole once more. With depot light-running this meant covering over 500 miles in the day, a high proportion being covered at motorway speeds.

The vehicles had Cummins engines and Voith four-speed gearboxes and these were, in our early days, subject to some unfortunate failures. The gearbox oil was only being changed at very long intervals, when, to quote Eric Watts, (who had a spell running the concern), it resembled oil in which chips had been cooked for far too long. Changing the fluid much more frequently and purchasing a better lubricant put an end to most gearbox failures on the road.

They also suffered from niggling faults, such as water or oil leaks, or failures of one of the various and numerous electrical circuits. I arranged for MCW to take the vehicles back to Washwood Heath and do some updating work either for no charge or at much reduced prices. Eric also instituted a nightly inspection of every Metroliner once it had returned to base, and so reliability did come to be very much enhanced.

To increase the scope of the business more midibuses were acquired, six coming from Yorkshire Rider, others being purchased new, and some new routes were opened. One of these using standard sized coaches was introduced on the 19th October 1987. Branded as the 'Town Tracker', it ran every two hours from Weymouth via Dorchester, Poole, Bournemouth and Lyndhurst to Southampton. Also, every two hours was a shorter service from Bournemouth to Southampton, to give a 60-minute frequency over the more profitable part of the service. Again, traffic did build up, but not as quickly as we had first hoped. The last endeavour was to commence a service with ex-London Country Leyland Nationals, from Bournemouth centre to the large housing area of Kinson.

The Nationals in their all-over green livery looked drab on arrival but were repainted in a new style. Roofs and skirts were in Charlie green, window frames and the below waist panels were white with a gold border separating the white from the green of the skirt. We began to repaint the coaches in a similar colour combination, and I had hoped that the arrangement might be widely adopted as it provided the basis of a group style livery, but still retained the historic colours of the various individual companies. Some Midland Red North (MRN) and some London Country South West (LCSW) buses were similarly painted but in the end the Chairman, who obviously had the last say in these matters, elected to keep the existing layouts. However, in the case of LCSW, a consultant was engaged to come up with some new ideas one of which was adopted, as was the amended name–London and Country.

We did, though, have one continual problem. In winter it was possible to recruit all the drivers we wanted but then passengers were much reduced. In

Branded buses. As mentioned in the text, Midland Red North gave 'brand' names to each of its various parts. Here a Plaxton-bodied Leyland Tiger, bearing its Hotspur identity, awaits departure time.

One of ten Dennis Falcon/East Lancs single-deckers which were new to London Country South West. Six of these passed to Midland Red North. G306 DPA, shown here is working the 2/12 circulars which competed with Shearings.

summer passengers were very plentiful, but drivers seemed as short as the proverbial 'hens teeth'. It was decidedly off-putting. There was, though, a nasty lurking all the while in the background, as the leases on the Metroliners expired after the contract with National Express, and that body indicated that no renewal would be forthcoming. It apparently intended to father a new concern, Dorset Travel Services, to take on the work this being based at the Mallard Road depot of Yellowbus.

A note in my diary indicates that on Friday 18th of November 1988 I went to head office to participate in a meeting with representatives of the National Express concern, and wrote under the details, 'End in sight for Shamrock and Rambler'. Another entry dated the Wednesday 16th April 1989, reads 'last day for Shamrock and Rambler', so presumably that was the last operational day, and then two days later I took the office staff out at lunch time to entertain them to a final and farewell meal. The Dorset concern might have been under the impression that with the disappearance of Shamrock and Rambler, there could be some vehicles going cheap, but if any such thoughts were in mind there must have been great disappointment. All the Metroliners were ferried to Cannock for distribution around the operating companies, whilst homes were found for all the other vehicles, including the 44 midis.

Mention of Cannock leads me to pass comment on, what was in my view, the jewel in the crown, namely Midland Red North. In 1985 this had a fleet of 258 vehicles. There were 20 Fleetlines and 15 Olympians, but these double-deckers were far outweighed by the single-deck establishment of 141 Nationals; 68 Leopards; 20 Leyland Tigers; and 5 MANs; but I cannot recall that the latter formed part of the acquired fleet, which then contained a posse of midi buses. Some of these had worked from a depot in Lichfield, but this had been closed from the time of takeover. The previous management had adopted a 'branded' policy, the vehicles and publicity etc being emblazoned accordingly:

Mercian covering the Tamworth and Lichfield areas;
Chaserider covering the Cannock and Stafford areas;
Tellus covering the Telford area;
Hotspur covering the Shrewsbury area;
Midland Red line covering Crewe area; (this was a later addition).

I have a note to the effect that Drawlane acquired Midland Red North on the 7th January 1988. The headquarters of the company were at Cannock, the premises being relatively new, and not all of the available space was in use at the time of the takeover, which was to come in very useful as will be recorded later in this narrative.

In the event the Company Managing Director at the time of the change elected to retire, to be replaced by the Operations Director from North Western, but before too long he returned to Liverpool being promoted at North Western to Managing Director. We also lost the Operations Director who was replaced by my son Christopher, who subsequently became MD, when a former member of the Leicester City Transport staff who had moved on took up the vacancy that then existed at Cannock. MRN ran very well and there were no apparent maintenance problems, although it had to be said that the Company was spread over a wide area and it was consistently profitable.

A repainted Leyland National for Midland Red North at Reigate. My idea was to have a common-themed Drawlane livery that retained each company's traditional colours, but it never came to be adopted.

A former London Country South West National repaired and repainted in what might have been a group style livery. One of several Leyland Nationals intended for the Bournemouth to Kinson service, it, sadly, did not have a long Shamrock and Rambler life due to events recorded in the text.

A selection of London Country Leyland Nationals are parked up in the premises which seemed to have a dubious future, possession-wise. Reigate garage was not in London Country South West ownership.

Midland Red North Leyland Leopard PSU3 with Duple Dominant body is shown inside the Crewe workshop.

A former Crosville Bristol VRT SL3/6LX with ECW body stands in the Crewe depot yard. This had been transferred to Midland Red North control.

An ex-Crosville Dodge 50 series minibus with Northern Counties body sports its new C-Line livery.

There were, of course, various fleet changes, an interesting one being the arrival of some ex-London Country Leyland Tigers which were fitted with Berkhof coach bodies. These were regarded as time-served, so Cannock removed the coachwork though the framing proved to be difficult, and the chassis were then dispatched to East Lancs to be fitted with that concern's revised single-deck bus body. Unfortunately, we do not have a detail record, but believe that about 41 buses of the type were obtained. Midland Red North also took four ex-Shamrock and Rambler Metroliners which found useful employment on the express commuter services working, for example, from Tamworth into Birmingham, saving some previous rush hour duplication in the process. It is useful to mention here that, by the standards of these times, a Metroliner was an expensive vehicle costing around £88,300, but they were big and complex double-deck coaches.

According to a schedule that Eric Watts drew up, MRN took 15 other ex-Shamrock and Rambler vehicles, comprising of nine midis, and six coaches. Three of the latter had an interesting history as they were previously in the fleet of Cynon Valley Transport, that concern having decided to sell the coach undertaking to concentrate on the running of local bus services, a year or two after my departure. MRN also took into stock some of the almost group-standard Dennis Dominators with East Lancs bodies, and later nine Falcons with the Gardner 6LXCT power units and 4-speed Voith gearboxes. The Company also later received six similar buses from London Country South West. It did, however, suffer one set back when, during the night in early 1992, a fire started somewhat suspiciously in the Stafford depot. As a result of that, 24 vehicles were either lost or badly damaged comprising 18 minis, two midis and four full size single-deckers. However, the Company ran a full service the morning after, and opened a new garage in the Queensville area that was later made permanent. Midland Red North quickly recovered and continued to march on. A rather different sort of acquisition came about in the January of 1988 when I was appointed a Director.

East Lancashire Coachbuilders was set up in 1934, but was not into bus body building until the 9th May 1938 when the Company was reconstituted and Messrs George Alcock and George Danson became Directors there. Both gentlemen had been previously employed in senior capacities by Massey Brothers of Enfield Street, Wigan, who were well-established bus body builders, so they brought their experience to the Company. They joined Mr Walter Smith, who had been involved in the original venture and who owned the property – Brookhouse Mill – where bus building began. The very first contract to be obtained was for ten double-deck bodies on Leyland TD5 chassis for Bolton Corporation Transport, and these received metal frames, a type of construction that the Massey firm would not undertake at the time. The Company continued to prosper, and was able, by one means or another, to manufacture bodies during the war to better than Ministry of Supply utility standard, and after 1945 it widened its customer base, working in the main for various municipal undertakings. In May 1970 it suffered a serious setback, when a goodly proportion of the premises were destroyed by fire with production being badly affected, but again this unfortunate occurrence was overcome.

One of ten bus-seated Leyland Olympians with ECW bodies which were split between Cannock and Tamworth Depots.

These two Dennis Dominators which were built to a reduced height joined two earlier vehicles on the C84 Chester to Hanley service. East Lancs designed and built a low-height body as suggested by the author (shades of Todmorden depot of 1971).

Walter Smith died early on, and the family retained his shares, but eventually in early 1964 Cravens of Sheffield, who had also been involved in body production in the past, took control of the Company. They then opened another unit, Neepsend Coachworks in Sheffield, that utilised Blackburn designed frames, but this was closed in February 1968. Ownership changed again, the John Brown concern – Cravens owners – taking control, which then passed to the Trafalgar House Group; that organisation decided to put East Lancs on the market, and so it came to pass into Drawlane hands. Obviously if a biggish group was to be built up, then having an in-house body builder was going to be of considerable advantage.

I was able to persuade Arthur Danson and George Alcock, sons of the two experienced original directors who now ran the Company, that a reduced-height double-decker could be a useful product and that a new single-deck body ought to be designed to look more modern than the existing one. I suggested that it should also have deeper roof edge coving panels that would be more attractive to our advertising contractors, and so hopefully provide better rentals. I also wanted to introduce the straight-run staircase based on a pre-war Roe design into group bodies, as had been used for Leicester vehicles.

The East Lancs staff could and did design virtually anything, this area being the province of George Alcock, when the works staff would put it all together. Here Arthur Danson kept an eye on output and also looked after sales, both gentlemen being the firm's Joint Managing Directors. During the time of my direct connection with the Company it built, or had on order, the following of vehicles for the Drawlane Group:

9 Dennis Dominators for London Country fleet numbers 601-9;
10 Dominators for North Western fleet numbers 630-9;
4 Leyland Tigers for Midland Red North fleet numbers 1916-9;
13 Volvo DD's for London Country fleet numbers 610-22;
14 Volvo DD's for North Western fleet numbers 640-53;
27 Leyland Tiger rebuilds for MRN fleet numbers 1710-36;
10 Dennis Falcon for LCSW fleet numbers 301-10;
8 Dennis Falcons for North Western fleet numbers 381-8;
8 Dominators for North Western fleet numbers 626-9/63-6;
6 Dominators for MRN fleet numbers 1801-6;
36 Volvo DDs for LCSW fleet numbers 648-65/7-84;
2 Dennis Darts for MRN fleet numbers 501 and 701.

Some of the MRN Tigers had bodies specially built to pass under two very low bridges at Little Haywood. East Lancashire Coachbuilders was a company well worth having in the group.

We did not, of course, acquire every company for which a bid was made, and two that came into this category were Southern National and the Red Bus Company based in Barnstaple. Before it was discovered that these two concerns had been acquired by their management, I had been looking over the ground and so came to the end conclusion that we could well be better off without them. There were too many empty miles between Weymouth and Taunton and in North Devon, those areas do not represent good bus country. The mention of Weymouth, though, leads me to leave buses for a few lines and go nautical.

East Lancs bodied 10 Leyland Lion mid-engined chassis for Nottingham City Transport, which were delivered in 1989.

Inside the Whalley New Road East Lancs finishing shop with the new Preston Transport Leylands in the foreground. I do not recall it looking so neat and tidy. This photo was taken when the company was in Drawlane ownership.

As group MD, I was able to press East Lancs to produce a more modern looking (for 1988) single-deck body, and here is the result. The deep roof cove panels were intended to be more attractive to advertisers and so command a higher rental. Midland Red North also took a series of these bodies which were fitted to former London and Country Berkhof-bodied coach chassis.

A new design. H501 GHA was the prototype Dennis Dart with an 8.5m East Lancs body. It proved to be a successful combination.

At the time of the Drawlane acquisition of East Lancashire Coachbuilders, an order was in progress for Cowie Group subsidiary, Grey Green. These bodies were mounted on Scania chassis.One of the two with coach seating for 75 passengers is shown prior to delivery.

Kingston-upon-Hill Transport took delivery in 1988 of six single-deckers with bodies by East Lancs. These were mounted on Scania N112CRB chassis and the bodies classified as dual-purpose with seats for 49. They were given fleet numbers 701-6.

The Drawlane ownership of Crosville resulted in competition with the municipal operator. In Chester bus station a Crosville Mini Lynx Metrorider and a darker green-liveried Freight Rover are awaiting their departures in March 1989.

Deregulation had caused some operators to reduce the size of their fleets by selling some relatively new vehicles. Also in Chester bus station in March 1989 are two council-owned buses, on the right is No.103, a Dennis Dominator with Northern Counties bodywork, which had been owned from new. Standing alongside is No.7, a Roe-bodied Leyland Olympian which had originally been supplied to West Yorkshire PTE.

From time-to-time it was necessary to go to the old NBC offices and sign up for a concern that was in the process of being acquired. On one such occasion, fellow Director Stanley McCardle and I were to do the necessary, and to avoid making a very early start elected to stay overnight in London. We had had our evening meal and were sat at a table in a fairly busy lounge, when we were approached by a seemingly very important individual who asked could he take one of the empty seats by us? We obviously said "Yes", and it was equally obvious that he wished to enter into a conversation with us. He turned to me first and asked where I came from, so I replied Torbay. He then asked me if I ever did any sailing. My response was that we did have an 18ft sailing dinghy, but my two children were the experts, as I was a dry land sailor. He went on to tell us that he was very keen, and began to explain how difficult it could be to sail from Weymouth to Torbay thanks to the tide race alongside Chesil Beach. One had either to carefully monitor the tide times or go well out into the channel and to then tack back towards Torquay Harbour, all this in considerable detail.

He then turned to Stanley, and asked where he lived. The answer was Salisbury, so the knowledgeable one indicated that Stanley was not likely to have been associated with boats and sailing, but Stanley gently pointed out that he done a bit in the past. The question was then posed, "Have you ever sailed from Weymouth to Torbay", when the answer was "yes, several times". Then came question two. "And what sort of a boat did you have then?" Stanley's reply was "An Aircraft Carrier", our friend's jaw dropped so much that his chin nearly cracked the table top, so he repeated in bemused tones, "An Aircraft Carrier!" Stanley replied in the affirmative and added the name which alas I cannot now recall.

However, I then thought I had better add a word or two, so I told our friend that Stanley had had a distinguished navel career. He had joined as a boy seaman at the age of 14 and gone to sea on the battleship HMS Rodney at 15. He had then worked his way up from the lower deck to be commissioned, to retire only a few years previously with the rank of Rear Admiral, so "yes" he had done rather a bit of sailing in his time. Our companion, obviously totally deflated, suddenly remembered that he just had to make a very urgent phone call and so left us in a rush, when I was of the opinion that I had just witnessed a truly delicious encounter. It is a tale well worth telling.

On the 17th March 1988, Drawlane acquired the business of North Western, but this was not the North Western Road Car Company based in Charles Street, Stockport of my earlier days. That North Western had had a fleet of around 524 vehicles, when on the 1st January 1972 the heart of it, in and around Manchester, was sold to the Greater Manchester PTE. The peripheral depots and vehicles that then remained with Charles Street, Stockport were then passed to either Crosville or Trent. A new coaching arm was set up as the remaining quarter. The new North Western had its headquarters in Hawthorne Road, Bootle, and had emerged from the slicing up of the large Ribble concern, which in 1985 had 887 vehicles. This North Western had depots at Hawthorne Road, Bootle in Liverpool, at Skelhorne Street where the coach station was also located, at Aintree and in Wigan. It had inherited a fleet of around 280 vehicles. Once again

Following deregulation many Sunday services were put out to tender and unusual vehicles and liveries started to appear in 'foreign parts'. The weekday service between Buxton and Manchester was operated by Trent but for a short period the Sunday service was operated by Drawlane's Crosville, as depicted in this view of DVL 490 (WTU 490W), leaving Buxton market place in 1988.

there were some changes in the top management, the Managing Director and the Chief Engineer taking up other positions but replacements were soon in post.

There is not a lot I can say about this acquisition. The vehicles were in fair condition, with no apparent engineering disasters lurking, in the back of the garages, but there were some important property developments. The original Crosville Company had been active in the Liverpool area, but ran into difficult labour problems. If my memory serves me correctly it had a depot on Edge Lane where the problem was centred. Eventually Crosville took out its 'locked in' buses in the dead of night, and effectively closed down its operations in the City. Prior to these unfortunate happenings taking place, it had been about to invest in a new depot at Love Lane which had much improved facilities, but this remained unused. Unused that is until Drawlane took it over, closed Skelhorne Street and Hawthorn Road, and transferred all operations from these places to Love Lane. Here I was provided with a northern office, which in the event I seldom used, but it was a nice thought. Later on the idea of closing Aintree also surfaced, but I was not involved in that process.

The new local management, after the Ribble cutting up, introduced quite a striking basically red livery with large blue triangles covering the nearside front and offside rear and some white relief and this was continued by the new owners, no North Western vehicle being repainted in my suggested style. The selling off of NBC concerns also came to include the former Crosville Company, which was split into English and Welsh portions. The English part passed to the ATL organisation, but the Welsh bus business remained on offer and I went to investigate the situation. In so doing I had at the back of my mind the gloomy contents of a report produced by the Crosville General Manager before the Transport Act became law, and when the concern had a fleet of 903 vehicles. In the report the GM stressed how right from the 'twenties Crosville had adopted a policy of cross-subsidy, the good mainly-English areas supporting the Welsh parts which in the main were far from lucrative. The report went on to suggest that if in the future the Company had to obtain its living from commercially sound areas, then the 404 buses working in Wales would be cut to 172, and 16 depots or out-stations in the Principality would have to close. I stress here though that no account was taken of the possibility that some tendered services might be bid for quite successfully. The English side was expected to do rather better, but here the forecast suggested that the then fleet of 499 buses might be reduced to 257, again ignoring any tendering possibilities. Most of the existing locations continued, although some could reduce from depot status to one of outstation form. I did a tour of North Wales, venturing into the more remote regions, and came to the conclusion that there were too many dead miles with plenty of sheep but few potential bus passengers, so I recommended that we gave this opportunity a miss when in any event none of us were Welsh speakers.

Eventually, though, the ATL concern decided to sell-on Crosville England and it came to be purchased by Drawlane as from the 13th February 1991. This was, of course, a different story.

The company at this time had depots at Birkenhead, West Kirby and Ellesmere Port, which between them had an allocation of 14 minibuses, 79 double-deckers and 9 single-deckers; giving a total of 102. Chester had 20 double-deckers, 3 single-deckers, 12 coaches and 20 minibuses; giving a total of 55. Northwich had 9 double-deckers, 18 single-deckers and 10 minis; giving a total of 37.

Crewe had 3 double-deckers, 3 single-deckers and 16 minis; giving a total of 22. Etruria had 9 double-deckers and 4 single-deckers, to give a total of 13. Runcorn did rather better with 19 double-deckers and 27 single-deckers, but that was an establishment that I have yet in 2013 to see. Warrington had 5 double-deckers, 12 single-deckers 5 mini buses and 10 coaches; giving a total of 32. Macclesfield and Congleton had been inherited from the old North Western Company and now shared an allocation of 16 double-deckers, 11 single-deckers and 18 minis; to give a total of 45. Bredbury, a quite new establishment, had 10 double-deckers, 2 single-deckers and 13 minis; to give a total of 25, whilst the Rochdale Depot, once the home of Yelloway Motor Services, was a base for 12 double-deckers, 3 single-deckers and 21 minis; or 36 buses in total Of the various bases, Macclesfield was regarded as satisfactory, but Congleton and Bredbury were basic outstations with Bredbury being particularly so. Birkenhead and West Kirby were quite acceptable, but Ellesmere Port was another very basic place consisting of a hard core surfaced parking area.

Northwich was also acceptable with a large parking area, but the situation at Crewe was unfortunate. The depot was regarded as first class, having very adequate facilities but had apparently been sold, and the former Shamrock and Rambler Chief Eric Watts, who had now become the Crosville Engineering

Manager, hoped that it could be repossessed. He was not impressed by the replacement out-station located on an industrial estate that again was of a hard core parking area, with a Portacabin providing facilities for the drivers. Chester had been modernised in recent years and so was satisfactory. Runcorn as a building was in the reasonable class but Eric expressed some concern as to the way in which it performed, and so felt that some re-organisation was called for.

Of the remainder, Warrington was far from ideal from a maintenance point of view, Bredbury was also basic consisting of a parking ground, whilst fuel was kept in an old road tanker without any form of bund wall, so if it did ever come to leak then the end result could well be costly. Finally, Rochdale had adequate pits and a suitable parking area, but it was only placed in the acceptable category. West Kirby was scheduled for closure on 31st December 1989 so was not assessed, Ellesmere Port was not felt to be adequate for its purpose, whilst Rock Ferry was regarded as perhaps actually more than good, ideal in fact.

I did, in the early days, visit several of the above locations, and with Eric I came to the conclusion that there was scope for the making of worthwhile economies, but I was not to have the time or the opportunities to become properly involved. The same reservations were to my mind also true of the traffic departments' place in the scheme of things because Crosville was not doing financially as well as it should have done. Investigation and planning for the future were called for, but again I was never involved in any such activities.

Before I severed my connection with Drawlane two other concerns were acquired. The last of these which I will comment on first, was none other than Midland Fox, which was intriguing.

I well remember the first Salisbury meeting with the Senior Officers of that company, where they expressed concern that I might want to make their life difficult in view of the relationships that had existed in my Leicester City Transport days, but I assured them that they had nothing to fear. That was in the past, now we were on the same side and it was the future that mattered. However, it was interesting to have a first hand sight of the Fox financial performance and note which were the best routes, and those that were marginal, when by and large my previous assessments were not all that far from wrong. I never did, though, become a Director of Midland Fox, but I did come to spend an interesting day in Leicester looking over the minibus workings which had been introduced after my departure from Abbey Park Road, and which had certainly given the succeeding management quite a lot to think about.

This leaves me to comment on the last concern in this catalogue – namely London Country South West. The London Country Services were, of course, set up by the London Passenger Transport Board to run routes which served the outer environs of the Capital, which also formed the longer distance Green Line routes. The vehicles were painted green, as opposed to the red livery adopted for vehicles working in the centre of London and its surrounding Boroughs. In due course, control passed to the later London Transport Executive, and this state of affairs continued until the Ridley 1985 Transport Act came into being to affect the Central Services. It was then passed into the hands of the Greater London Council, where responsibility for London Country and Green Line work were transferred in 1970 to the newly formed National Bus Company. It must have been an interesting concern to manage in this revised form, with some 1,115 buses in the fleet which consisted of 356 double-deckers, 493 single-deckers; and 266 coaches working from 23 garages.

It was the M25 of bus undertakings, stretching as it did right around the London area, in fact the M25 basically ran through its operating territory, and this state of affairs continued until the Ridley 1985 Transport Act entered its several stage journey that would turn it into law. The edict now went forth that by the 1st September 1986, it had to be broken up into digestible proportions and this duly took place. Four operating companies were formed, each having a share in the Greenline network together with a fifth part known as Gatwick Engineering Ltd.

Around this time the original one-piece concern had not been doing too well financially, so the Managing Director elected to stay with what became known as London Country South West. This concern, with 415 buses, a headquarters and garage at Reigate, with other depots at Addlestone, Godstone, Staines, Dorking, Leatherhead, Guildford and Crawley, was acquired by Drawlane in the February of 1988. Presumably the Managing Director had had thoughts of mounting a management buyout, but if so, lost out to Salisbury, and did not stay long with LCSW after the takeover.

In a book published after these events it was suggested that my involvement in LCSW was intended to ensure his departure, but nothing could be further from the truth. His home was on the north side of London, his office far to the south, so his commuting journey must have been far from easy. He took the opportunity to take up a position nearer home, and I am sure that if we were able to meet again after a lapse of many years we would have the friendliest of conversation. There would be lots of reminiscences about our times as Technical Assistants with Manchester City Transport, and the name Crossley would be frequently heard.

LCSW territory was to me totally unknown so I was taken on a tour of the area and its garages, which unfortunately were not Company property. Their freeholds were acquired by the Speyhawk concern from the NBC, with the agreement that they were to continue for bus housing purposes for some years to come, thus finding some alternative accommodation was prominent in Drawlane future planning. In the event, Staines and Dorking closed in March 1990, Chelsham in April 1990 and Reigate – where the size of the office had been halved – in October 1990. Croydon gained a new garage in the period. Nevertheless, all this occurred after my departure so I was not involved in the associated work.

I did, though, quite soon become aware that meeting output requirements was to become difficult. I came to see the MD this particular morning, who was at the time talking to his senior lieutenants. I was invited into his office and sat in an armchair reading my paper until the meeting came to an end, but after overhearing part of the conversation I moved up to sit at the table. Later that day we went to Staines where some out-of-use buses were parked up due to a shortage of skilled vehicle electricians, so I contracted with a former LCT supervisor, who had set up his own business, to bring them back into use. He was then kept on for some time to help with repairs at other garages. This, though, was only for starters. After the MD had left for his new north-side position I held a watching brief for some time, and in this period actually became Chairman of the Greenline Group, something that I could never have imagined.

One night I was staying in the area and decided to go for a few bus rides. These took me further than I had first intended and so I found myself in Addlestone feeling famished as I had had little to eat during the day. I was quite close to the LCSW garage so I decided to visit the canteen and purchase some refreshment. I duly entered the building, went to the counter and asked for a pot of tea and a sandwich, but was not challenged or asked who I was, which I found surprising. I went to a table in the corner of the canteen and began to have my snack, being part way through it when a driver obviously on break entered. He began to tell his 20 or so colleagues in the canteen that the bus he had been driving was not fit to be on the road, and needless to say he was not restrained with his comments. I waited until he had finished and then asked him if he knew who I was, when the answer was in the negative. I then introduced myself to one very surprised employee, who began to apologise for his rather pithy observations.

I told him not to worry about that and I addressed myself to those present saying that I wanted the complainant and about six other staff members to come with me. I intended to drive the offending Leyland National for four to five miles, but I was not familiar with Addlestone and as it was quite dark needed a guide to take me to a place where I could turn round without difficulty. We trooped into the yard and boarded the vehicle, I sat in the drivers' seat and started the engine when one of my colleagues came to stand by me and directed me on a suitable route. I suppose I did cover about 4 miles before returning to the garage. Once there, I told the assembled company that I was in full agreement with our friend's strictures. The vehicle was horrible. It was full of rattles, was a poor performer, and gave the positive impression that its suspension system was notable for its complete absence.

I then said it would NOT go into service again until it had been fully overhauled, and that I would be back in Addlestone the next morning to test a few more Nationals, and so it came to pass. I did not blame company Chief Engineer for this unfortunate state of affairs. He was simply short of skilled craftsmen as the LCSW wage rates were way below those that were then being paid at Heathrow, Gatwick, or other local establishments. However, there was no doubt that if a Department of Transport Vehicle Examiner had laid his hands on some of the buses that I went over that morning, the problem that existed in meeting peak hour output would pale into insignificance. Immediate stop notices would have been issued on a confetti style scale, and Addlestone was not alone with this sort of problem. I checked a Park Royal-bodied Atlantean at Godstone when sitting in an off-side seat in the centre of the lower saloon, and I could push the whole side outwards as the adjacent main pillar had become detached from the supporting under-frame cross member. Fortunately relief was ready to hand.

At Cannock, Midland Red North had that spare space, a large depot yard, and the ability to recruit craftsmen. I told MD Hilditch to take on several fitters: a body maker or two; some painters and a vehicle electrician. As soon as the staff was in place, an average of two LCSW vehicles per week were ferried to Cannock prior to requiring their annual test; after overhaul they were returned to Reigate to pass first time, and two more were received at Cannock to undergo rehabilitation. The cost involved, chargeable to LCSW, was around £3,000 per time but this was cheaper than what would have been involved locally, and by securing first time passes the Department of Transport came to think that LCSW maintenance standards were almost beyond question.

The work continued until, in January 1990, the new Managing Director decided to move maintenance back in-house, dispensing earlier in the process with the services of the Chief Engineer, which I felt was rather unfair but it was not then my place to interfere. I did, though, register objections to his wish to buy Volvo City Bus double-deckers instead of Dominators, and also to acquire a first batch of Leyland Lynx single-deckers. My objections to the former were based on positive experience. A horizontal engine in a single-decker was in life terms from 85% to 90% worse than a comparable vertical engine, even though the latter was carrying a much heavier double-deck body. That battle I lost, and 40 City Buses with East Lancs bodies were placed on order, but I cannot tell you if my fears did eventually come true, nor do I know how their fuel consumption compared to that of the Gardner-powered Dominator. Nevertheless, I did win the Lynx argument; why buy outside-sourced bodies that at first had a dubious reputation, when we had a very good producer of our own in East Lancashire Coachbuilders?

I must say though we did not exactly agree that he did a very good job in sorting out some acute labour relations problems, but his stay was not over long. After I had left he was told that London and Country was to be split into two, each with its own Managing Director, both being existing senior staff members, when there would be no place for him which was to say the least very hard.

LCSW at the time of the takeover was certainly an interesting company and one that was not easy to run. Its stage carriage services were affected by the considerable increase in the car population in what by-and-large was a very affluent area, but fortunately it did possess some routes that were very worthwhile operating.

To my mind the best money spinner of them all was the Speedlink Service that connected Heathrow with Gatwick or vice versa. This was of the 'premium' form. There was, at each airport, a lounge area where passengers who wished to make the transfer were kept in comfort and supplied with hot drinks whilst they waited for their coach – never ever a pure bus – to arrive. They were then escorted to it by the hostess, helped with their luggage and then whisked off in considerable comfort to their destination at a single fare of £10.00. I spent some time at either terminal being surprised by the number of passengers changing from one airport to the other, and I also travelled on the vehicles when I had time to do so. No wonder the former Managing Director 'bagged' LCSW Speedlink and the other airport services.

I never came across any cause for complaint, but towards the end of my association with Drawlane Speedlink was divorced from the then London and Country undertaking. It was re-titled Speedlink Airport Services Ltd and placed under the control of its own Managing Director, who had previously been the Traffic Manager of the combined concern. The suggestion was then raised that the coaches were not as clean as they might be, and that maintenance should be improved, but again I was not to know if there was truth in the allegations, and if so what would be done to put things right.

Midland Red North opened up minibus operations in Derby using midi vehicles. Here former Shamrock and Rambler staff member Brian Laws, now depot manager, stands in the doorway of his new charge. It was, surprisingly, successful.

I must say, though, that my involvement with London Country South West in my initial days did much to improve my geographical knowledge of its operating area, which previously had so far as I was concerned bordered on being totally foreign territory. In later days, the two new parts of London and Country were subject to considerable re-organisation, and the Speedlink operation passed to the National Express concern that was then under McEnhill control.

From the moment that I first met Ray McEnhill I came to like him. I felt that he had a sense of humour and could be mischievous, teasing his subordinates by telling them that he was going to pursue some line of action which was certainly not the case. There was no doubt that he was exceedingly clever at spotting opportunities, and that would provide a financial advantage. I felt that inside him there was always a kindly streak present, seeking for a way to emerge. I also felt that our relationship in the early years of our association was just about as good as was possible. Certainly at Christmas 1988 he had written to me, thanking me for my effort on behalf of Drawlane, a letter which contained a very sizeable cheque by way of a totally unexpected bonus. The amount certainly caused one of my Board colleagues, who was not so favoured, to express a few disgruntled words. Then after Christmas he told me to go and order a new Jaguar, passing my Rover to a staff member lower down in the pecking order. That 3.6 well-equipped Jaguar was delivered to my home on the 14th January 1989. However, things then began to change and perhaps the catalyst formed around the events of the 31st January.

I had suggested to Ray that we were about to meet a diplomatic problem. We were due to take Crosville over on the 13th February and here came the problem. The Crosville and Warrington Transport depots were cheek by jowl and their relationships since the passing of the Transport Act were not of a high order. Warrington was a very good customer of East Lancs, almost to the point of placing 100% of its order with Blackburn, so would it not be a good idea to tell the Warrington GM in strict confidence what was in the wind, and indicate that whilst competition was the name of the game, it might be possible in the future with a bit of good will each way to avoid treading on each other's toes.

Ray thought the problem through and agreed this was desirable, so I journeyed to Warrington and did the necessary. After our chat, the GM took me to look at Warrington's bus station that I had never seen and returned me to his office where I picked up my car and left for my next port of call.

He then went back to the bus station, where a Crosville inspector asked him who was the man he had been showing around, so my name came to be mentioned. On the 1st February a furious Ray McEnhill asked me why I had gone to Crosville's Runcorn Bus Garage, and there he revealed information that was strictly confidential. I told him that I had never done any such thing; I did not know where the garage was; and had never even seen it; which remains the case to this very day. Obviously someone, (but who I don't know), was bearing false witness against me and I repeated word for word my conversation with the Warrington GM. I then tackled him to be assured that he had not in any way betrayed the confidence I had entrusted to him, so how had this most regrettable situation come to pass? Ray came to realise that I was telling the truth, but our relationship never quite seemed the same and so I was not surprised when he asked me to call on him on the 27th of June.

He then began to tell me what he had in mind for me, but I only listened with one ear as I lifted up my brief case onto my knee, opened it and took out a single sheet of paper. Then using the bottom of the case as a desk, I signed and dated the sheet, placed it on his desk and said, "I suggest you read that". He adjusted his spectacles, read it, and said, "This is your resignation". I confirmed that indeed it was, saying that I had noted how the wind was blowing of late, I felt sure that my usefulness to Drawlane was at an end, and so it was time that I jumped ship. His response was rather odd. He indicated that the sheet was of no use to him, and if he took it then he would have to put it in the safe, so would I take it back. However, I had offered three months notice so we had a deal. He then asked would I in the meantime carry on as of old, but not mention to anyone else the arrangement we had arrived at.

For the next three months nothing more was said and I did as he had suggested, but on the last day of September after staying overnight on the outskirts of London, I was up early so I had the Jaguar valeted and then drove to Endless House. He had a visitor on my arrival but eventually the man, who was a stranger to me, left and I slipped into the office to be greeted with, "Hello what can I do for you?" I replied "shake me by the hand", as I placed the office and car keys plus the company credit card on his desk. I added that I had now completed my three months notice so it was time to say cheerio, shake him by the paw, and leave for Paignton and retirement.

His response was to ask me to stay on as a Drawlane Director and retain an interest in East Lancashire Coachbuilders. I ought, though, to retire from the boards of the operating companies.

He further suggested that I could work full or part time on my existing salary, but if I say worked for two days in a week then I would be given 40% of the full weekly rate, but now came the last bit, which had been obviously thought through. He was of the opinion that my son Christopher and I had in his words, "broken the mould". We had set up a mini bus operation in Derby, opening a depot on 31st July, putting in 30 mini buses with a peak vehicle requirement of 27 and recruited a former Shamrock and Rambler supervisor to act as depot manager. This was doing quite well under overall MRN supervision, so he asked if I would go and look for other places where the exercise could be repeated?

Now, it so happened, that as a Drawlane Director I was in receipt of private health insurance, and that was a facility that I could now usefully use, whereas if I resigned on the spot it would not be available to me. I decided to think of myself, and so said I would give the idea a try. I was then missing for around four weeks, but on my return, still possessing operating company directorships, I went out prospecting. I chose Norwich as my first site of endeavour, as I had of, course, often visited the city in my Great Yarmouth days.

I then summed up the end result; this was not going to be a part time assignment. One would firstly have to draw up a list of potential mini bus routes and decide how many vehicles would be needed. Then a suitable garage would need to be obtained, and staffed with drivers, administration personnel, and maintenance men. The Derby base was within fairly easy reach of Cannock and Crosville's out-stations whilst Bredbury and Rochdale were also in striking distance of some principal home depot, but a great deal of travelling could well be involved here and winter was coming on. This was certainly not for me, so it was going to be, "Goodbye Drawlane", in the near future.

The Drawlane Board agenda for the 4th December 1989 had on it the item, 'Composition of the Board', and when that item was reached, (Ray McEnhill not being present on the day), I stood up, put my papers into my brief case, and said "Good morning gentlemen, this is where I leave", and so I did.

I was asked if I would wish to go home in the car, but said "no" as there was a good train service to Exeter, nor later would I accept any payment for outstanding holidays etc. I left 'clean' and in view of what was waiting for me round the corner, I was very glad that I had.

Moral as Thomas Wentworth Earl of Stafford said, when he heard that King Charles 1st had signed his death warrant after saying it was something he would never do, "Put not your trust in Princes". Or as Arthur Danson told me, "In this world you are only as good as your last balance sheet". I cannot fault that.

4 – Life After Death

Not very long after I had retired from the Drawlane Transport Group, I was sat in the lounge reading one morning when the phone rang. I picked up the receiver to find the Town Clerk/Chief Executive of Leicester City Council on the other end of the line, which certainly was a surprise, only that surprise came to be quickly compounded.

He started the conversation by saying that his attention had been drawn to a piece in one of the Transport Journals, which indicated that I had retired from my Salisbury commitments, so what was I currently doing? The answer to that question from a work point of view was exactly nothing. Question two then followed; had I retained any Drawlane share holding? The answer to that one was "No", but then I had never, despite numerous promises, ever been offered any shares. Then came the major surprise. He asked me if I would come to Leicester at some convenient but early date, as certain Members of the Council wished to see me? It seemed that the Transport Company was not doing too well, needed a Chairman who knew something about running buses, and would I be interested in possibly accepting the post?

I said that I would make the trip, but I was not going to drive 224 miles to Leicester, attend a meeting, and then drive a like distance home again, so I would need one night's accommodation. I was told that this would be no problem, and as I was free from any other commitments, I left it to him to tell me the day and time when my presence would be required. He duly rang back a day or two later, and so on the 19th January 1990 I started up the car, and headed for the Grand Hotel, left the vehicle in the park and walked to the New Walk Centre, to discover as much as I could of the reasons behind the invitation. I was again told that the Company was not doing well. The previous MD, who had latterly also acted as Chairman, had left and a company doctor had been brought in, initially in a consultant's role, but had seemingly not made much of an impression. He asked would I now have a try at endeavouring to achieve viability? Interestingly, this same gentleman joined the Board as Director on 19th April 1989, only to resign on the 9th May 1989, one must wonder why. I thought for a few seconds, decided that this was a challenge that I had to take on, and so I said "Yes".

Consequently, on the 1st February, I walked into the Abbey Park office via the back door, and so came face to face with the lady who, from my earlier days, had acted as the receptionist. She expressed some surprise at seeing me and asked how I was, but became even more surprised when I told her that if anyone wanted me I could be located in my old Committee Room corner. Needless to say she asked why, so I explained that I was back as Company Chairman, when she said rather hesitantly that no one had told her! I'll bet her phones were busy after that exchange, but no matter. Now, to say the concern was not doing too well was the understatement of the year. It had started to trade on the 26th October 1986, when to fund the transfer of assets from the City Council to the Company, shares to the value of £483,000 were issued, with a debenture of £138,000 also being raised.

As a group it came to own three active parts, namely: Leicester City Bus (LCB) doing mainly what Leicester City Transport did of old; Leicester City Bus

Engineering, mainly repair of Council vehicles; and Loughborough Coach and Bus, set up in July 1987. The last unit came about following the purchase from Trent Motor Traction of its depot in the town, and some of the local services operating therefrom.

I then discovered a very illuminating document dated the 8th March 1989, compiled at the request of the City Council by Price Waterhouse, which provided a financial review of the then company situation. At that date the fleet consisted of 200 Leicester or Barlestone-based buses, with 15 midi buses being allocated to Loughborough. The Accountants went on to point out that there was a very competitive situation in the City, with LCB having about a 6o% share of the market. On the 31st December 1988, accumulated losses of £2,046,000 had whittled the original share capital down by 40%, and losses were continuing at the rate of £100,000 per month. It appeared that the Members of the Council, who had been original Board Members, had resigned their seats in February 1988 since when two Executive Directors, the company secretary, and two Senior Managers, had in effect been running the enterprise. Of the first three, the former MD who had latterly also acted as Chairman, had resigned in early March 1989, and now the shareholders were recommended to bring in a Company Doctor to try to pull things round. He might well not be from the Transport Industry.

As it was, it was estimated that by the 31st December 1988 there would be a loss on the part-year nine month working out at £1,158 which certainly gave me a dubious inheritance. The review went on to say that Loughborough operations were a financial disaster, there being a nasty gap of £38,000 between income coming in, and expenditure going out. So advice was, "Sell it off as quickly as possible", as adding in indirect costs the loss equals £26,600. When the books were closed on the 31st March 1989, the loss on the group amounted to £1,306,000, which when added to what had gone before, meant the accumulated losses were now up to £2,195,000.

The fleet now consisted of 179 double-deckers, 18 midi buses, and 6 coaches. Quite a number of buses had been sold to raise much needed funds of £600,000, and a contract with Dennis had had to be renegotiated. This had called for 13 complete buses per year to be delivered over five years, fixed prices ruling for the first two years. The first two batches were received in April 1988, and March 1989, but the suppliers were told the 1990 batch could not be accepted and the 26 due over the following two years would have to be cancelled.

In actual fact, I knew all about this sad story from my previous capacity as a Director of East Lancashire Coach Builders Ltd, and had told MD Arthur Danson that there was no point in flogging a dead horse. If the Company cannot pay, let it off the hook without penalty, but tell the Directors that in return for this good turn we expect to be in pole position if, or when, more new buses are being contemplated.

Now I had to start work, when economy had to be the order of the day. However, the Company Doctor had come into the picture in May 1989, and under his guidance, or so it appeared, a suggested long-term business plan dated 3rd August 1989 had been placed before the shareholder, but in my view it never had a chance of succeeding.

The idea was to sell off Rutland Street where, as previous thought, had been to use the building for head office purposes, around £90,000 of expenditure had been incurred in carrying out various alterations. Now the intention was to rent a small Head Office which would have a very limited staff somewhere in the City Centre. The Abbey Park Road site would also be sold off, and three new depots brought into use being located – so the plan proposed – in Hamilton, another in the Beaumont Leys area, and a third around Blaby or Wigston. Barlestone was to continue as of old. Beaumont Leys was to be the replacement Central Depot where all major overhaul work would be undertaken. Each Depot was to have a manager who would be responsible for developing services in the area which his vehicles were to serve, and every one, (Barlestone excepted apparently), would be provided with about 15 midi buses to offer competition to any other predatory concern.

The plan suggested that expected capital expenditure to build and equip the three new establishments would cost £5.937 million, whilst funds to be generated by the sale of existing assets could be in the order of £7.746 million. In addition, selling off the testing station and the LCB Engineering arm should raise £75,000 and £100,000 respectively. This to me seemed rather like pie-in-the-sky. No land was earmarked for constructional purposes, and so there was no provisional planning consent either. Additionally, where was the money coming from to buy the sites, and then pay the building contractors? One could hardly move out of Abbey Park Road and plonk around 200 buses on the street whilst it was sold off, and the money used for the purposes outlined, but here, according to my reading, something was missing.

Under the rules appertaining at the time, if a company sold off a worthwhile site within its first year of existence, the whole of the proceeds resulting had to be passed to the original Council owner. If it was sold off after the Company had been in existence for 10 years, it could keep the whole of the monies so realised. In respect of intermediate years a sliding scale was to be adopted, so if all this could have come to fruition in the fifth year of LCB's existence, then it could have kept half of the cash, resulting from the disposal of Abbey Park Road and Rutland Street. However, the plan went on to forecast that do all this there should be a cash surplus of £1,984,000.

I soon found that several people had been recruited to fill positions in these hoped-for peripheral locations, and so, as it was never going to happen, I found myself with the unpleasant task of making them redundant and trying to give them some financial comfort, for they were in no way to blame for the misfortune that came to be theirs.

The closing of Rutland Street did go ahead though, on the 13th May, being sold eventually to the City Council when a new and later useful feature emerged. The union said that as there were no longer canteen facilities in the city centre, the staff would need to travel to Abbey Park Road for refreshment, and this must cut into their break times. As a result, two shuttle buses were to be provided linking the city with the depot, to provide as fast a transit as possible between the two locations.

I had to take a quick overview of the situation that presented itself to me, and I made two early decisions. The testing station generated a lot of cash, although recent uncertainty had resulted in a drop in income. It was now not going to be

Competition. The scene at the Beaumont Leys loading point in Charles Street. The Kinch ex-London Fleetline was not a bad bus but performance-wise it was completely outclassed, and as Gilbert Kinch said to me one day at this very stop, he had never expected our vigorous response. After making life more difficult by opening a second front on our Rushey Mead service, he finally folded his tents and left to look for profits elsewhere. Now why could he not have looked to do battle with Midland Fox?

A Kinch ex-London Fleetline muscles in on Citybus's lucrative Rushey Mead service, number 21. Note the Fleetline painted in-situ destination display. The attack commenced on 4th January 1993 and ended on 23rd April, Citybus having responded in an effectual manner.

sold, and the word to that effect was passed by the staff to our customers. Very, very, fortunately, the number of tests began to rise back to something approaching previous levels and even beyond, so that in the financial year 1992/3 15,522 tests were undertaken.

It was obvious that redundancy costs would have an adverse effect on the accounts for the year in which they arose, but after some twelve months substantial savings would appear. These were certainly needed as there were substantial overdrafts with each of the Company's two bankers, and one of these was making rather alarming suggestions that an early repayment of the sum owing would be appreciated.

Not everything that the interim management had done, ie from 1989, had been bad, rather the reverse in fact, so that on the 31st March 1990, the consolidated profit and loss account showed that the loss for the year had been reduced to £480,000. It was recorded at £1,306,000 twelve months earlier, and £480,000 was in fact finally reduced still further after certain exceptional items had been included. Of the £118,000 here involved, some £97,000 had resulted from the sale of Loughborough garage, the Loughborough involvement being the subject of much pungent comment by the authors of the report produced for the edification of the Council in March 1989.

Initially Trent Motor Traction had a fleet of ten midi buses located in the town, but these cannot have been as viable as that Company must have wished, as it decided to withdraw. The then LCB management obviously thought it could do better, and so took over the local operations as from the 13th July 1987. They acquired 11 midibuses which were leased from their supplier, and recruited 17 drivers to do the necessary. The buses were based at premises owned by County Travel, a firm with which the original LCT had had good relations in pre-deregulation days.

County, seemingly, sold out, and so LCB operations moved to the former Trent garage at the 'Rushes', a building which, with its requisite plant, was purchased for £348,355 in January 1988; but now the scale of the business began to look very different. What had been a part-day operation blossomed into something far more substantial; bus allocations rose to consist of 18 midis and 5 double-deckers, with staff levels also increasing to 38. A further enlargement took place in May 1988 when the Trent Barton subsidiary pulled out of Stamford. LCB then opened an outstation in the town and provided it with 3 single-deck vehicles. Sadly these innovations proved to be financially horrendous.

The loss up to the 31st March 1987 amounted to £189,000, and to £265,000 in the nine months to the 31st December 1988, making a total loss of £454,000. There was only one thing that could be done, and so on 30th January 1989 the Board resolved to close down Loughborough and Stamford activities, and seek to realise the assets that should become available. However, this would take time, and a loss of £243,000 was anticipated by 31st March 1990. It was all a very sorry story, but fortunately was not going to involve this author to any substantial degree. In the event, the staff level at the 31st March 1989 of 676 had been reduced to 614 by the 31st March 1990, with the attendant and quite significant payroll savings. Now, on the 1st April 1990, I had only been in office for some two months so had had little time to make any impact on the on-going situation, but it was very obvious that there was much to be done, and so one prominent question was "Where do I start it?" I was soon favoured with more than a few suggestions.

In May 1990, the then Operations Director resigned, and his place was taken by a gentleman who had been recruited back in the days when those three peripheral depots, plus Barlestone, had been management intentions. Despite the uncertainty that he must have experienced, he had obviously been studying the situation, and so presented me with a twenty page document that set out all the areas within the operations department that he felt could render some degree of economy, if some successful trade union negotiations could be achieved. This was something that needed careful study in view of certain local complications though.

Firstly, some time earlier when the financial situation was more than a little bleak, Management had been successful in negotiating an economy package with the Trade Unions which certainly did provide some worthwhile savings. For example, before its implementation, sick pay make-up monies had been paid after only one day of absence, now the waiting time had increased to three full weeks, whilst holiday pay had also been affected. There was, of course, more to it than is set down here, but one very significant clause has to be mentioned. The employees side made it clear that if Company finances began to improve to a worthwhile effect, then it would seek the reinstatement of the former working agreements.

Secondly, the Labour Force had declared its intention to acquire the LCB Group if at all possible, and, with this intention in mind, had set up the City Employees Buyout Team or CEBOT for short, and had entered into a partnership with another former municipal company to help it towards achieving success.

Here was an awkward complication, as official instructions to the Board were to assist CEBOT as fully as possible, but at the same time protect the interests of the Company to the full. This seemed to be a classic case of having to serve, or at least try to serve, two masters, one being the existing shareholder, the other a party that wanted to become just that. It soon became obvious, however, that CEBOT and partner had neither the financial or management resources to make it happen, and so it came to withdraw from the scene, but not before the Company had funded an outlay of £20,000 in 1991/2, which covered payments relating to research that had be done on behalf of the would-be purchasers.

To return to our Operations Director document, 'proceed with caution and don't set the River Soar on fire' was my guiding philosophy here, or as my father had said earlier when telling me of his experiences in the field of labour relations, "Never prod a sore place, (or should it be a Soar place), if you do not want to provoke an undesirable reaction".

Operations were not, though, the only area that required a good coat of looking over, and so a great deal of my time in the 1990/1 financial year was spent in meetings of one sort of another, and trying to plan for a more advantageous future. At the same time, I obtained a suitable flat not too far from Abbey Park Road – much cheaper than spending four or five nights a week in a hotel. I simultaneously closed down the one I had retained up to then in Aberdare, and moved the furniture etc into the new location.

A Dennis Falcon and a Metropolitan outflank a Kinch competitor on a city loading point as a company Iveco heads for East Park Road.

The Northern Counties-bodied Falcons had a different front end design to those built by East Lancs which, with a different white paint layout, made them very easy to identify.

On test. Number 622, shown here, was one of three Dennis Falcons, Nos.620-2, which entered service on 15th February 1993. Gardner 6HLXCT turbo-charged engines were fitted, so there was a lack of 'urge'. Northern Counties 48-seat bodies were carried. The usual Voith 3-speed gearbox was also present. Four more identical buses, Nos. 623-6, were delivered in May/June 1993.

Secondhand. No.763 was one of four Renault/Dodge S56 vehicles (Nos. 762-5) fitted with Perkins 4-cylinder engines and Chrysler torque Elite automatic transmission. 762 and 763 had been new to Greater Manchester Transport and went into service with Citybus on 1st August and 1st July 1992. The other two followed on 1st March 1993. The Northern Counties bodies seated only 19.

Let me digress for a few lines though, and proceed to describe an event that brought some unexpected light relief and humour into my life, at a time when it was rather badly needed.

The calendar year 1991 did not start well for me, as I was ill over the Christmas holidays. I had to visit the Doctor and then found that I would have to undergo an operation, so on the morning set aside for that purpose I was lying in my room feeling rather glum, when the door opened and a truly breathtaking nurse entered. "My name", she said, "is Laura, and I am here to prepare you for the operation, and then to stay with you all day, and make sure you have a good recovery". The diction was impeccable, but there was an odd accent apparent, so I asked her where she came from. The answer was from Germany, when she added that she did not like Germany all that much, as the people she had been with were so serious and quite devoid of humour, so she had come to England to finish her training. I asked her how she liked living in Torbay, and was surprised when she told me it was OK, but she preferred the north of England. I asked why, and what area did she prefer, to be surprised again when she told me she had friends in Halifax, and that was where she would like to be. I asked her in which part of the town did her friends reside, but she could not remember so I began to say the names of the various outer districts, for example Mixenden, Illingworth, Warley etc, until I reached Siddall, when she said that was the place. I further inquired did they live on Backhold Drive or Jubilee Road? The former was the correct location, so I then I asked her what she said to her friends when they first met up. Looking rather puzzled, she said, "Hello of course", so I asked why she did not greet them in their own language. This puzzled her still more, so I explained that when two friends met in Halifax the first to speak would say, "Nathen then how art ta. I'm noan so bad mysen".

For the next half an hour, as she did indescribable things to me, we rehearsed these words, but it was too good to last and two porters appeared with a trolley to convey me to the operation theatre ante-room. I was put to sleep after the Doctor giving me the anaesthetic managed to find a suitable vein in which to insert his needle. I started to come round about four hours later, when I became aware of my cheek being lightly tapped, and as I slowly opened my eyes it was to become aware of that gorgeous face looking down at me, when from her lips came the words "Nathen then how art ta. I'm noan so bad mysen". Well I had asked for it, but I confess she got the better of me in the end. I have to say she did brighten a rather painful day, leaving me in the early evening when sadly I was never to see her again.

Driving the 224 miles from home to Abbey Park Road was not on for some time, but at last I was sufficiently fit to resume duty, being none too pleased to find that whilst I had been away my Board colleagues had negotiated a Wage Award, that in my view was over generous in view of the ongoing financial situation. However, there was nothing much I could say, especially as not too long after I was personally responsible for putting up the cost of operation, and in view of what transpired later it was a very good job that I had.

First though, we reached the 31st March 1991, closed the books on the year and reviewed just how we stood. At first sight, a loss on the group of

£510,000 was a matter for serious consideration, but it was made up of three items that were worthy of close inspection. Firstly, exceptional items. The total figure under this heading was £229,000; £24,000 of which covered the early withdrawal of certain, very unreliable, mini buses. Then £181,000 was paid out to cover enhanced redundancy funding, mainly administrative posts having been abolished as a result of the complete closure of the marketing and personnel sections. We did, though, realise that employment law was becoming ever more complicated, and so we recruited a professional who knew far more about the subject than the Board Members did. He continued to offer advice and guidance whenever the need arose, through the rest of my period in office. At this time though there were increasing signs of better days ahead.

Twenty four Metropolitans had been taken out of service, each one representing an immediate saving due to their high fuel and maintenance costs. In addition to this, as mentioned before, Rutland Street had been closed from the 13th May 1990, all operations now being centred on Abbey Park Road; however, the attendant savings were in part offset by the agreement to introduce those canteen shuttle buses with all their attendant running costs. Put together, these things resulted in a group operating loss of £196,000, which was certainly an improvement on what had gone before.

Withdrawal of the Metropolitans and the Optares meant that new buses had to be obtained, and these materialised, in part, as six East Lancashire-bodied Dennis Falcons that came into stock from the January of 1991, as fleet numbers 611-6, and proved to be a very fortunate purchase. As the financial situation did not permit our buying them on a cash basis, they had to be leased, but the terms of that lease were arranged so that they would be paid for when they were exactly half way through their book lives, so we were not mortgaging fleet future to an undesirable effect. Two Northern Counties mini buses, fleet numbers 751 and 752, were acquired in the December of 1990 under similar terms, more were to follow later. We thus came to enter the 1991/92 financial year looking forward to more prosperous times, but in life one ever knows just what problems lie in wait around the corner, and one of these was totally unexpected.

Towards the end of 1991, we arrived at the time when various Road Service licenses were about to fall due for renewal, and so the necessary forms were filled in, I signed them, the appropriate cheque was issued, and the documentation was sent off to the office of the Traffic Commissioner, who was now located in Cambridge – the former Nottingham Office having been closed. No new licences were issued though. Instead, a curt letter was received, indicating that the Commissioner was perturbed by the apparent parlous state of Leicester City Bus vehicle maintenance, and so required the Company to appear before him in Public Inquiry to answer for its sins of omission, and this could turn out to be a serious business. Fortunately, I had by this time been in office long enough to reach some decisions prompted in part by my riding on the buses when in service, and prowling round the City Centre watching them when at work, and this had led me to various conclusions.

A revised inspection scheme had been introduced in October 1991 on a ten-working-day basis, working around fleet numbers. So on day one, buses 1, 31, 81, 201, 231 etc, were checked, when the inspector did nothing but inspect, it

A second generation Dennis Falcon with Voith close-coupled gearbox, No.613, stands at the Beaumont Leys terminus. A Kinch Fleetline is behind with two further Citybuses in company livery behind it. City services 74, 75 and 76 left for the city centre from this location.

Number 756 was part of the eleven midibuses in the series 751-61. These were based on Renault S56 chassis with Perkins 4-cylinder engines and Allison automatic gearboxes. Northern Counties 25-seat bodywork was fitted. 754 went into service on 27th January 1992, the others on various dates between 751 on 1st December 1990 and 761 on 14th September 1992.

being the task of other staff members to put right any defects that came to be recorded. The 'two's' followed, then the 'three's', and so on, until it was one's day again.

A section of the former tramway shops fronting Abbey Park Road had been reopened, and in them were located a paint shop, and a body repair unit, which was dealing with one vehicle a week when new bearers and floor could be installed, and other major work carried out. Up to two buses a week were repainted in new Imperial red and cream livery. We had also started a blitz on catching up on seat repairs or removing graffiti, for the fleet was showing all too many signs of suffering from excessive vandalism. As a result I decided to embark on a new Court tactic. We would not employ a solicitor to put up our defence, instead I would front our response, and take with me some of the staff who could give evidence to the effect that whatever had occurred in the past was NOT happening now.

We travelled to Cambridge on Tuesday 11th February. I told the team what to expect as they had never been involved in Traffic Court procedure before, and the following morning we took our places in the Court Room for the stipulated 10.00am start. The Commissioner, Brigadier Compton Boyd, in his opening statement did not mince his words. He had 'DRACONIAN' powers at his disposal, and would not hesitate to use them if the need became apparent. Old-established concerns, such as LCB with previous good records, should never have been allowed to get into the state that had resulted in them being called before him. The first, and as it happened, the only witness for what I will call the prosecution, took the stand. This was Vehicle Inspector John Leyland. He outlined a full catalogue of failures stretching over a period of some two years. For example, in November he had placed stop notices on two vehicles that had come straight out of the workshops, one having a fuel tank leak, the other having no less than six dangerous defects. He added that there had been a 28% failure rate, but a dramatic improvement had been noticeable from the end of 1991, and this was continuing. He finally concluded his statement and the Chairman asked me did I wish to question him. He seemed rather surprised when I replied in the negative, saying that I accepted in full every word of Mr Leyland's evidence, but all this was in the past, things had changed, and so I turned to my team and asked that the members might be enabled to give their evidence.

They consisted of Eric Watts, who had been brought in to act as Engineering Consultant, Maurice Dames, the Services Officer and former Body Shop Foreman, Joe Walls, the new Paint Shop foremen, Ray Kersley, the Works Convenor, Mike Yeomanson, and Examining Mechanic and the then Engineering Director, Alan White. They all did brilliantly, describing how thanks to the improved financial situation parts could be obtained from suppliers on normal commercial terms, instead of it being a case of no cash no parts, morale had improved and maintenance was now of a high order, for Mr Leyland had inspected 12 vehicles of late, finding no defects at all.

The Commissioner finally retired to consider his verdict, but his deliberations were not of long duration. Returning to Court he congratulated the team and the Company on its efforts, and said he now had no doubts as to the way in which

Dennis Dominator, No.152, wends its way through the city centre on the route to Mowmacre Hill. New on 7th April 1989 it was the last of the batch purchased that year, in the later to be cancelled contract. Based on a Dominator Mk 6 chassis, it was powered by a Cummins CL10 engine, as were the others in the batch, Nos. 140-52.

A Metropolitan repainted into Company colours, No.175, stands in one of the former tramway bays. A repainted Dennis is in the background, whilst two other buses in Council colours complete the scene.

LCB buses were being maintained. He could not, however, excuse entirely what had transpired in earlier years, and so he was issuing a severe warning that nothing of the sort must occur again. For the future all the road service licences would be reissued for a full five years, and the Company, which on this date had 213 vehicles, could retain its 220 licence discs.

Finally, I invited the Brigadier to visit Leicester on some early date convenient to him, meet the team again, and see on the ground the work that was being done to keep the buses in full working order. Rather to my surprise, he promptly accepted the invitation, and on 24th February came to Leicester and spent a goodly part of the day with us. A member of the staff, (not from management), took him round, and he met with one exception those who had given evidence in Court earlier. Before he left, he told me how much he had enjoyed his visit and how refreshing it was to meet the skilled staff who actually kept the buses running. The day marked the beginning of a friendship that was to last until his untimely death at far too young an age.

There was though a sequel to this that made me wonder. The week after our appearance in Court the Midland Fox Company had to answer to its maintenance sins in Public Inquiry, but representatives of that concern had come along to Cambridge on our day and had listened to all that had transpired. I did, therefore, wonder if they had learned a few tricks from our performance, but be that or not as it might be, it came to suffer from some of Brigadier Boyd's draconian powers and had both its fleet size and licence disc holdings reduced.

This brought us up nicely to the 31st March 1992, and when the books were closed, our earlier grounds for optimism became clear. During the year the staff level had been reduced by a total of 30 posts. Administrative personnel had reduced from 92 to 58, which was indicative of the over heaviness of the office establishment, but conversely in order to improve the condition of the buses eleven more men were being employed in the workshops, bringing the relevant figure up to 122 posts, out of a total of 553. Earlier in the year, a flat payment of £50 to each employee had been negotiated in return for improvements in working efficiency, and a further modest pay rise was negotiated for introduction in the April of 1992. To offset this, a fares increase was introduced on the 22nd of March, but in the event this did not bring in as much as was anticipated. That was something to be considered as the new financial year wore on.

Further 1991/2 economies had seen the conversion of two former double-deck routes to mini bus operation with the helpful reductions in fuel and manning costs. The end result was certainly an improvement on anything that had gone before, as there was a group profit of £153,000. In actual fact, Leicester City Bus returned a surplus of £180,000, whilst LCB Engineering returned £151,000, but these healthy figures were offset by exceptional items expenditure of £178,000, of which £168,000 was spent in funding the aforementioned redundancies. Another pleasing factor here was the reduction in the accumulated deficit, this dropping from £3,067,000 to £2,914,000, whilst the figure of 'cash at bank' also showed a considerable improvement. These improvements prompted the Council to announce that LCB was not for sale, but coming events led to the reversal of that decision.

In view of the foregoing financial results, one could have thought that the

In the paintshop. Early in my Company days an improved paintshop was opened in the former tramway works that fronted Abbey Park Road. Here, under enthusiastic chief Joe Whall, buses were quickly turned out to the excellent standard shown here.

Off with the old, on with the new. Dominator No.252 in the City Council inspired 'City' livery stands beside a sister vehicle, No.141, in the Imperial Red and cream Company colours. Note the subtle changes in front styling of the latter to make a one-piece front upper screen.

Midibus No.718 was one of 23 Iveco/Carlyle 25-seat vehicles, Nos.715-37, obtained via a hire purchase agreement. Nos.715-26 were new in February 1989 and Nos.727-37 followed in December of that year. All were fitted with Fiat diesel engines and Iveco synchromesh gearboxes.

A full view of the Council inspired red, white and grey livery as applied to one of the single-door Metropolitans that represented my first and last such purchases. A design that was short of sufficient development work, it at least kept MCW in business and provided operators with new vehicles when the British Leyland group, thanks due to plant mergers and closures, simply could not. For that, at least, the industry had to be grateful.

Directors were expecting better times in 1992/3 and perhaps they were, only with some reservations. It could be anticipated that thanks to the redundancies that had been made, more substantial benefits would accrue, and passenger levels might not be subject to dramatic shrinkage as the local competitive situation had appeared to stabilise.

Some time before I left the Drawlane Group, that concern had acquired the Midland Fox business which was not exactly a money spinner, and despite my departure and later that of Christopher Hilditch, who was now the LCB Engineering Director, relationships with the Drawlane Principals remained on a friendly basis. One could perhaps say that a state of watchful neutrality had come into being, but one adverse and very significant factor had materialised.

The City Council had to put its refuse collection service out to tender, offers had come in, and a firm by the name of 'Sitaclean' had acquired the work. This concern had its own in-house full maintenance facilities, and so the refuse collection vehicles that had been repaired at Abbey Park Road were no longer to be seen on the premises. This was not good news. Refuse collection vehicles have a hard life. They start and stop almost every few yards, and the materials they carry, plus their packing mechanisms, are subject to heavy wear and tear. Much repair work is necessary and this was, to Abbey Park Road, a very lucrative business. But now take a peep into the future.

Around this time, give or take a vehicle or two, the Pool Shop faced the following work load on behalf of the City Council.

Ground maintenance machines – 81 – Contract ends 31-12-94

General purpose vehicles – 364 – Contract ends 31-12-94

Street Cleaning machines – 39 – Contract ends 31-12-95.

It was obvious that when these contracts had run their course the City Council would call for competitive tenders, and unless it became possible to reduce our costs to those appertaining in the private sector, the work would go elsewhere. In 1991/2 this business had made the very useful contribution of £150,000 to the coffers of the company, and its loss would be serious, leaving Abbey Park Road with an unused portion of the premises with all the requisite plant and equipment remaining in situ. What alternative business could be obtained? That was a question that had to be put to the test.

The new financial year started off quietly enough though, and from the provisional figures provided at the earlier Board meetings in the year, it seemed that profitability continued to be realised and nowhere more so than in the MoT Testing Station. This had suffered previously from its apparent uncertain future and a shortage of testers resulting in some work having to be turned away, but now both problems had been resolved to such an extent that the level of business now being done was such as to forecast a profit of around £10,000 being forthcoming by the end of the financial year. Before that point though, three problems, two that could never have been anticipated and one that might have been, arose with an adverse effect on finances. Numbers two and three in chronological order came into the unexpected category.

Number one arose in August of 1992 when the Company's advertising contractor Primesight went into liquidation, leaving LCB with a bad debt of £20,000, and ensuring that no further advertising revenue would be forthcoming for the next few months. Fortunately, a new company 'Bus Advertising' came on the scene and took the work over from the 1st November, promising a minimum of £70,000 per annum by way of rentals in a full year. It is often said that plastering bus panels with adverts results in a very unsightly vehicle, and sadly, especially with 'all over' advertising, this is often the case. But what concern can afford to ignore this sort of revenue?

Taking them further out of chronological order, surprise three became all too prominent when towards the end of October the Municipal and Mutual Insurance Company, a long-established concern, closed its doors for good. LCB had been paying some £31,000 per annum in premiums, but whilst it was possible to negotiate alternative cover, our new insurers called for a premium of no less than £70,000 for the year. In view of its lack of experience with our on-going performance, it was of rather little comfort when it added that if we had a minimum number of claims then we could expect a more advantageous price for 1993/4. By the time that this little shock was being felt though, the surprise that might just have been expected was working against LCB's well being.

This not altogether unexpected piece of nastiness arose on the 1st October 1992. Some time earlier Gilbert Kinch had sold his Wreake Valley business to Midland Fox, when it was agreed that he would not operate any competitive services in or around the City in advance of the above date. However, having acquired several ex-London Transport Fleetlines repainted in a blue and cream livery, he began to run a ten minute day time frequency from the Charles Street loading point to Beaumont Leys, competing almost directly with LCB's 54 service that served this growing part of the area. The only basic difference was that the Kinch buses left the City via St Margaret's Way, whilst LCB left via Abbey Park Road. There was only one thing to do – double our frequency to reduce possible Kinch concern income to a minimum – and here we did have two advantages. We put it to the Trade Union that, thanks to a much improved frequency, no one was going to have to wait for long to go to and from the depot canteen, so the shuttles would be withdrawn, and the two buses with all their associated costs would now be used for commercial/competitive purposes.

Secondly, we would run the route with the new Dennis Falcons. Falcons 617-9 entered service in December 1992, numbers 620-22 followed in February 1993 and 623-6 arrived in May/June 1993. Renault mini buses Y53-61 took the road over various dates in 1992. A final four, numbers Y47-50, made their debut in April/May 1993. Now there was not much wrong with a Fleetline, I had run lots of them in the past, but their power-to-weight ratio did not compare to that of the Falcons with their single-deck lighter weight and their Gardner 6HLXCT turbo-charged engines. As Mr Kinch came later to remark to me, when we chanced to meet up in Charles Street, he had never expected such a strong response – but then did he think we were going to lie down and let him cream off day-time traffic, leaving us to provide the far from lucrative early morning, late night and Sunday services?

This, though, did not discourage his concern's efforts, and so on the 1st December 1992 that first incursion into LCB's ribs was extended to Beaumont Lodge. Then, to increase competition still further, as from the 4th January 1993,

The original Leicester City Transport Ford coach is in Abbey Park Road yard. Never a lover of lightweight vehicles, it was not to be long in the fleet after my arrival. Its purchase opened the door to much increased coaching activity and the acquisition of a whole fleet of high specification vehicles, (Spacecars excepted!)

After my return to Leicester as Chairman/Chief Executive, I had the first Dominator restored to its original livery, complete with appropriate legal lettering. Here it stands alongside a new Company Dennis Falcon. I was glad to hear, as I wrote this book, that No.233 continues in preservation.

Kinch buses began to run a ten minute frequency over another of LCB's more lucrative routes, namely the 21 service that linked the City Centre with Rushey Mead. Again, Kinch operations were confined to the more advantageous parts of the day, leaving LCB to continue with the rest of the daily or week end timetable.

Once again our frequency had to be increased to counter the opposition, and it also became necessary to adjust fares on both this and the 54 service, matters which obviously cost us money. In the event it may have been that the Kinch concern had tried to do too much, as the 21 incursion only lasted until the 23rd April 1993, when competition thereon ceased thus providing LCB with four buses that could be used elsewhere. My thoughts turned to wondering how we might provide even more competition on the 54, but in the event nothing of the sort came to be introduced as a more fundamental problem began to surface, namely just what future does LCB have?

The subject was raised within the Board. I asked the Members to go away, and come back in another week or so having thought about suggestions they could make which would improve the financial position of the group, and also what were their views about trying to mount a purchase bid. One member was firmly of the opinion that the speaker would not be prepared to become involved, the others together with the Company Secretary were generally in favour if the attendant risks could be reduced to a minimum. So question one was, 'What value should one place on the enterprise bearing in mind that the 'claw-back' condition still remained in situ and would effect monies one might try to realise from a property sale?' Here some very tentative investigations put a value of £1,600,000 on Abbey Park Road and one of £230,000 on the Barlestone property, which not too many years earlier had been provided with a new office block. The old private company workshops remained with most of the vehicles being parked out of doors on hard standing. After thinking things over, the conclusion was reached that a figure of £3,250,000 was the maximum that might be considered but could this ever be possible?"

It would, with a squeeze, have been possible to raise the £250,000 so £3,000,000 would need to be borrowed say over ten years at 10%. This would mean paying down capital at the rate of £300,000 per annum, with a like amount of interest arising by the end of the first year. LCB had never made anything like this amount of money, (£600,000), in its years of trading to date so was there a way in which one might reduce the loan debt?

It had become very obvious that the Traffic Staff union was very much against any management purchase proposal coming into effect, having recommended its members not to attend any meeting management might call to explain what might be involved if a reasonable proportion of the shares were allocated to the employees. However, perchance the Union Officials had done some arithmetic of their own based on earlier CEBOT calculations, and so had realised the extent of economies that would have to be made to ensure that LCB could keep to the conditions that would enshrine the receipt of the requisite loan figure.

Forecasting the future never can be easy, but we undertook an exercise and came to the conclusion that if competition was to remain as it then was, the testing station did make the sort of surplus anticipated and we retained a similar amount of work in the Pool Shop, then a small surplus could be forthcoming. Nevertheless, there was much uncertainty around, and so I suggested to the

To prevent the promotion of the 'cult of the individual' (sounds like Soviet Russia) in 1984 the council decreed that the names of the Departmental Chief Officers had to be removed from all local authority vehicles. When the original Dominator, No.233, was repainted in original livery in later Company days, the old legal lettering was restored along with the city coat of arms. This photo was taken on 25th August 1992.

The initial prototype Dennis Dominator. The East Lancs body structure was one of those 'purloined' thanks to the ready co-operation of Managing Director, Arthur Danson. It was never taken into Leicester stock.

Council that the Members might consider putting the LCB Group on the market.

The Council came to a speedy decision, making the announcement in February 1993 that the undertaking was to be sold, recruiting the well-known accountancy firm of Price Waterhouse to act as sales agents. That concern produced an Informative Memorandum, or sale prospectus, to give a possible purchaser an initial idea as to what they might expect for their money. If, of course, their bid proved to be successful, facilities to undertake the necessary process of 'due diligence' would be made available. It was stated in the memorandum that indicative offers should be in the hands of the Sales Agent by 5.00pm on the 14th June 1993, when those of interest would proceed to stage two with an exchange of contracts taking place by the 31st August, but in the event this timetable was not realised.

Whilst the foregoing moves were afoot, the existing Board continued to manage the affairs of the undertaking, and more economies were put in train, and usefully so, in the Engineering Department.

By now, only the last five single door Metropolitans to be purchased remained in part day service, as did virtually all the rest of the double-deck fleet. Off peak and Sunday services were worked by the Falcons on the main lines, with midi buses elsewhere, and this reduced the fuel bill per week by something over 25% which represented a very sizeable saving.

Some redundancy affecting unskilled and semi-skilled staff took place, but all the skilled staff were retained with night shift activities being re-organised. A charge hand was appointed, and he and those working on nights with him became unit exchangers, when the subject to receive the shift's attentions and the parts required were placed together by the vehicle lifts, so that there need be no delay in commencing operations. This proved to be very successful, improving overall vehicle availability first thing in the morning. Sadly though, all was not well within the Board itself.

On Monday 19th April I was scheduled to travel to the north of the country to attend an annual transport conference. However, my train did not leave Leicester until mid-morning, so I had time to call a quick Board Meeting to set out one or two possible suggestions for future progress, to be considered whilst I was away, (for about four days), and telling the longest serving member of the Board that he would be in charge whilst I was absent. I duly reached my destination, to be surprised and shocked when I took a telephone call from him in my hotel later that same evening. He then told me that after consulting certain colleagues and the Company Secretary he had suspended from duty another Board member pending my return to the office. I do not intend to comment further here on this very time-consuming and unfortunate matter, so let it be sufficient to say that it left us with an atmosphere that we could well have done without, an atmosphere that was to last for the rest of my days in office, although they came to be few in number.

On the afternoon of Wednesday 22nd August I had a visitor, who indicated that it would be better if I was not around whilst the sales process continued, and so I should go on leave forthwith. I burst out laughing when I received this news, saying that it must be something of a transport industry record to be removed from, what was in effect, the same office of the same undertaking not once but twice, but thus ended my association with Abbey Park Road with a little qualification.

Surprisingly, I did not feel at all disgruntled by this piece of news, leaving for my flat in high spirits, but that feeling did come later, only was not to last long as this narrative will come to show. Although the times were not exactly propitious, we had done some work on the possibility of putting in a bid for LCB. This involved finding a financial concern that would have been prepared to back us with a loan to the extent of £3,000,000, on the terms indicated above. We teamed up with Trevor Smallwood and his colleagues, who were successfully running what was then the independent Badgerline group, prior to it later forming a part of the now well-known First Group. We discussed what might be possible with Badgerline, and were working on the basis that LCB would be affiliated to it, but would still remain largely independent. After discussing the pros and cons of the situation, we could not be said to be enthusiastic about our prospects, but Trevor and his Finance Director gave us some good advice having, of course, masterminded their own company purchase. We noted that First Group had recently purchased what had been Northampton Corporation Transport, and did seem interested in taking over LCB, and then perhaps putting the two together in a single management unit.

Then on the 31st July I received a letter from Leicester, telling me that I was now no longer on leave, my services having been terminated, and now came the disgruntled bit. We went to Abbey Park Road one afternoon with our Badgerline friends, to endeavour to ask some pertinent 'due diligence' questions, when the gentleman who had been put in to run the place 'pro tem' began to provide us with some answers in a very cooperative way. However, our presence must have been noted and acted upon, as we were then asked to leave the premises without delay, and so our tentative efforts came to an abrupt end.

In the event this for me was the best thing that could have happened. Over the preceding four or five weeks I had begun to think that there was something wrong with my wife, who would do or say things that were quite out of character. Being now largely at home all week, I could clearly see that all was not well, for in no time at all those early symptoms of Alzheimer's Disease rapidly progressed, and all too soon it was clear that she could no longer be left to live in the house alone. I looked after her for the next four years plus, but it just is not possible to give someone 24-hour care all day every day, and in the end I had reluctantly to agree to her transference to a suitable care home where she was later to pass peacefully away. Thus, it became obvious that even if LCB had continued as a Council-owned undertaking, I could not have remained as Chairman/Chief Executive beyond late September/early October.

This was not quite the end of the matter, as some work was done to see if it would be worthwhile setting up a small unit that could provide the new purchaser with some new competition on two or three of LCB's best routes, but these endeavours were never very serious. The cost of obtaining premises, maintenance facilities, staff, and vehicles could be easily ascertained, as could the cost of any mileage then introduced. However, assessing income levels was certainly an inexact science, and in any event, my increasing domestic responsibilities meant that I could never become involved in such an enterprise.

What did happen? On Friday 12th November, LCB was sold to First Group, the surviving members of the Board being told the previous day that their services were no longer required. I have never seen in print the price that the purchaser paid for LCB, but I have been told that the figure was no less than seven and a quarter million pounds, which may or not be true. If it is, then a very inflated price was paid, and the City Council can congratulate itself on securing a most acceptable deal. There is though a straw in the wind here.

When Trent Motor Traction sold its Loughborough operations to LCB, it was part of a deal that covered Trent acquiring 250,000 ordinary shares, or some 6% of the capital of LCB. In addition the agreement gave Trent, (or Wellglade, its holding company), the right to become the Council's first choice purchaser, unless LCB was sold direct either to the work force, the management, or work force and management in combination. Presumably, if the fictitious Central Midland Bus Company had put in the highest bid of say, £5,000,000, then Trent could offer £5,000,000 and so automatically take control. Here it would seem that the Trent Principals, put off by the amount the successful purchaser was prepared to pay, waived its right and walked away from taking LCB into its fold.

Perhaps I should add here that Trent never did receive any Board reports or was able to put a nominee on that body, but Trent representatives always did attend each Annual General Meeting. It would be interesting to know just how the purchaser fared financially with its new acquisition burdened, as it must have been, by the price paid which almost certainly was more than the debt outstanding on LCB at the date of my departure, but that is something we will never know.

Since those long-gone days of 1993, I have paid just two visits to the City of Leicester. The first was when my old school held a reunion for former pupils who had come to live in the East Midlands. For old time's sake I did go and look at the Abbey Park Road complex, now rather reduced in size thanks to the fire that had destroyed the former Pool Shop. As had been anticipated, the City Council had to follow the compulsory tendering procedure when the vehicle repair contracts came up for renewal, Abbey Park Road lost the work, and the associated part of the premises was let out for storage, when the materials put in it were unfortunately of an inflammable nature. Several members of my former staff saw me outside the premises, and suggested that I might care to step inside and have a look around, but I declined the invitation. I had no wish to renew old memories on site, and in any event, whatever was going on therein was nothing whatsoever to do with me.

The second occasion was on the 11th September 2011. I was scheduled that Sunday to go to stay with friends in the north of England but decided at very short notice to leave a day earlier, stay overnight at the Grand Hotel, and then on the Sunday put in an appearance at the Leicester Historic Vehicle Heritage Trust's Annual Running Day. Finding the hotel proved to be quite a problem, as the street pattern is rather different to what it was in my day, and the difficulties were not eased by the extensive road works that were then in train but that is another story.

On my way to the venue on the Sunday morning, I drove along Abbey Park Road and paused to look at the scene of desolation that now exists where the bus garage, former tramway works, and the 1930s office block once stood. Replaced by a smaller establishment on Abbey Lane, the owners would presumably have had no problem in realising the full proceeds of the sale, as the earlier restrictive 'claw back' clause would now have run out of time. I did not go to look at the replacement, but from what I was told by some of my former staff who came to speak to me, LCB's direct replacement now only operates about half of the number of buses that were once located at Abbey Park Road.

I much enjoyed my morning with some old friends looking at some beautifully restored buses, but I could not help nursing a rather guilty feeling, as the majority of those that I saw had been taken out of service, and sold to new owners, or worse, possible scrap during my period in office. Sadly too, no Dennis Dominator put in an appearance, but I was promised at least one ought to be on display in 2012.

Thanks to 1993 events in Leicester, and my ever increasing domestic commitments, it seemed at the time that the Passenger Transport Industry and I had parted final company after an association that had covered over fifty years, but any such assumptions that I might have made were very wrong, for the wheel had still to turn the full circle.

The offices at Abbey Park Road, Leicester, when under First Group ownership, has the 'For Sale' board displayed above the main entrance. The buildings were later demolished.

The impressive architecture of the main entrance reflects the civic pride which was often shown by the operators of municipal trams and buses.

5 – Completing the Circle

Those of you who have read my three earlier books will recall that in them I made reference to spending most of my boyhood years in the Saddleworth village of Delph; it was then firmly planted in the West Riding of Yorkshire. From even earlier years though, I had been attracted to trains, buses and trams, having always been blessed with a good memory. Now, years after, I can clearly recall riding on an Oldham tram to Grains Bar, and seeing the single-deckers at their West Street terminus, looking very old fashioned with their open platforms, before they left again for the restrictive Mills Hill Bridge and thence Middleton. It seems now that given a fair wind, and barring any misfortune, I might just be able to ride on one of the new Metrolink trams in that same place during 2014. I also remember riding on the Oldham Karrier and Guy six wheelers that in my first days in Delph, around 1931, worked the service to Oldham and Manchester, continuing from that City to Gatley, an extension that did not long serve the passing of the 1930 Transport Act. Like many boys, I had a bicycle, and would often ride it around the village pretending that I was driving a real bus, when the Delph and District Bus Company had a series of well-defined routes, over which it travelled, almost, but not quite, to timetable.

Due to my wife developing Alzheimer's Desease, I could not entertain thoughts of further work after I left Leicester, and this state of affairs lasted for several years when I looked after her at home. Believe me, Alzheimer's is a very cruel disease, and you can have no idea of the trauma it can cause until you experience its ravages first hand. Eventually, the professionals said that I had to stop looking after her, or else I too would become ill, so with great reluctance I consented to her being moved into a Care Home.

By the time this had taken place my son had joined, at first two friends, later only one, in running a small bus company located on Ward Street, Chadderton. This had a small but modern fleet of 20 vehicles, consisting of –

6 Dennis Darts with UGV bodies,
3 Optare XLS Intercity buses,
1 Plaxton Super,
5 MAN Varios, (3 long, 2 short),
5 Dennis Darts with Wright bodies second-hand from the West Midlands PTE.

These vehicles worked on a mixture of commercial and Greater Manchester PTE tendered services, and one of the latter involved working some evening journeys from Delph to Ashton-Under-Lyne.

Consequently, on the night of 6th September 1999, I drove my car to Delph, parked it up, and boarded the waiting Universal vehicle, sadly making no note of its identity. I then took it to Ashton, and as I journeyed through the familiar King Street, then Millgate, and the Sound, to pass the building that was once Delph Station to gain New Road, and so proceed via Uppermill, Greenfield Roaches, Mossley and Stamford Park to the Ashton Bus Station terminal, it occurred to me that the wheel had truly completed the full circle.

Here I was with a full-sized passenger vehicle, in which I had a financial stake, so that boyhood pretence had finally come true. By this time, Christopher had left Universal to take up a post with the Stagecoach organisation, leaving

When I came to live in Delph in 1931 the Gatley-Manchester-Oldham-Scouthead-Delph-Uppermill service (started on 15th May 1929) found work for Oldham's eight Karrier three-axle single-deckers, which were not exactly known for reliability.

The other side of the circle, ie Oldham to Uppermill via Lees, was worked by the North Western Road Car Tilling Stevens vehicles as per this typical example dating from 1928. Despite only 4-cylinder petrol engines, crash gearboxes and no front brakes, they were, at least, reliable, so much so that in the mid 'thirties, many were rebodied to last to post-1939-45 wartime days, although mechanically unchanged.

Two Universal buses are pictured in the Ward Street, Chadderton depot yard. Universal had a modern fleet of 20 vehicles.

Two of the five second-hand Dennis Darts with Wright Handybus 34-seat bodies and Northern Ireland registration plates were new in 1991. Like the other Darts they had Cummins 6BT power units and Allison automatic gearboxes.

Universal Optare XL1150 with a Cummins 6BTA-160 engine and an Allison automatic gearbox stands in the Wars Street yard. The body had 42 seats and standing space for 25 passengers. It was in service on 10th September 1997.

Two Dennis Darts with Cummins 6BT engines, Allison automatic transmission and UVG 31-seat bodies stand alongside a Universal Optare XL. The Darts date from August 1997.

me to continue as Chairman, having Power of Attorney over his shareholding. However, I was beginning to find that making frequent 286 mile trips from home to Ward Street was becoming rather too much for me. Consequently, I was rather pleased when a third party made an approach with a view to buying our shares. The approach made it very clear though, that there would be no place in the intended scheme of things for our existing partner. We felt we could not ignore his interests, and so we said that if he would pay a single pound more than the figure on the table, we would pass our shares over to him, and he would have sole control.

This he did, and so on the afternoon of the 15th December 1999, having reached full agreement, I resigned from the position of Chairman and set off for home and retirement. It was just as well too that I did, hardly reaching Paignton before I had to surrender to the worst bout of flu I have ever known, that laid me very low for far too long. So I ended my career in the Transport Industry at the age of 73. It was one for that for most of the days I thoroughly enjoyed, when it was a pleasure to go to work. There is no doubt that lucky is the man whose work is his hobby, and that was certainly the situation in my own case.

I now look back on the days covered in the four books of Steel Wheels and Rubber Tyres, and think just how fortunate I have been! From steam engines, trams, trolleybuses, and every sort of motor bus, from minis through to double-deckers, to articulateds.

Could any Transport Enthusiast ever ask for more?

I referred in volume one to the model Sentinel Steam wagon which arrived on my fifth birthday. A Sentinel promotional model to assist sales of their new SE44 and SE6 designs. How did one come to appear in a New Mills toy shop window? It was made in Germany and was about 20 inches long, finished in a brown and buff colour. I have never seen another one, or indeed another illustration. Peter Hilton found this one in a toy record book circa 1930. It was clockwork powered with a battery illuminated ash pan. I wish that I still had it!

The Bit At The End

It was my practice in my transport days to often take myself off for a bus ride or two to see what was happening on the system when I often found that the conversations of my fellow travellers was oft time just as interesting and entertaining as the ride its self.

This proved to be the case one Saturday evening. I had been out and about for two or three hours and now found myself sitting on bus number 328 which was preparing to depart from Keighley, the last departure of the day for Halifax.

For the record bus number 328 was one of the six ex-Todmorden Leyland Leopards of 1969 being fitted with a 43-seat Pennine body, and was now allocated to Elmwood Garage Halifax.

Like most Saturday last buses in this era it was already well filled, being just short of a standing load, but as we still had a few minutes to wait before departure time was reached I had begun to think that I would have to give my seat up to a fare paying passenger and then travel as 'staff'.

The lady who was sitting close to me was obviously having thoughts about the loading situation as she came to remark to her husband, "This bus is nearly full I wonder how many people it can carry?". Her husband thought knew the answer and replied in rather superior tones, "It's there, with a gesture towards the fleet number positioned on the rear of the driver's bulkhead, "328, thirty two seats eight standing". "Oh" replied his spouse, "I often wondered that those numbers were for." Well, I had seen an undertaking where the route number blinds were set to show fleet numbers, but this was certainly a new interpretation.

Travelling by bus could certainly widen one's education, even on a Saturday night in Keighley.

My first bus arrived in my bolster case (no stocking for me) at Christmas 1931 and my friend Peter Hilton searched through his record books to find this illustration of it. Of German manufacture and was some 14 inches long. Its tin-plate construction reflected the design of contemporary single-deckers with tram-style ventilators, no glass in the front near side windows, short rear platform and excessive rear overhang, a feature banned by the 1930 Construction and Use Regulations. The toy had adjustable steering and a powerful clockwork motor.

Only six of these units were ever made and here is a mystery. One certainly arrived at Leicester after my departure and had a single test run after being fitted to a Dennis Dominator. It was then, seemingly, returned to Gardner, but Paul Gardner tells me that there is no trace of its arrival at Barton Hall Engine Works. So if, reader, you know of the whereabouts of a Gardner 5LXCT I am sure there are people who would like to know.

Comparison of the five- and six-cylinder Gardner engines.

5LXCT	6LXCT
170 bhp at 1850 rpm	230 bhp at 1900 rpm
8.7 litres	10.45 litres
758 kg	908 kg

The Bigger Bit At The End

It is now almost fourteen years since I retired from the Transport Industry and in that time quite a number of references to my name have appeared in various publications, usually commenting on my activities or in odd cases lack of them.

Most frequently, are references to my association with the Dennis concern or Hestair Dennis as it then was, and certainly it gives me some satisfaction to think that the 'horse' I put my faith in is still alive and producing bus chassis, being the sole remaining British manufacturer, but its survival in the early days seemed to be by no means certain.

One day in this period the Company Managing Director received a call from a very high Leyland Group executive who invited him to come and have lunch with him at Leyland's headquarters as they had something to talk over.

John Smith duly accepted the invitation to find himself with not one executive but two when the sponsor of the event indicated with some arrogance, typical of that time, that Dennis DID NOT make buses; it produced refuse collection vehicles and fire engines. Leyland was the bus producer with some 93% of the market and that was how things should and would stay.

His listener was not to be intimidated by this expression but went on to point out that if such was the case then some competition was badly needed and this the Guildford firm was going to provide, and so it did.

It was a source of some later surprise to me that such a small factory, as it then was, contained such a wealth of engineering talent, and reader remember here that Dennis produced the Dominator, getting it well nigh right first time and then went on to design two versions of the Falcon with close coupled or remote mounted gearboxes, the Dorchester underfloor-engined chassis and the Lancet with a vertical engine mounted in a similar position. Each of these was then developed, viz. the Dominator which could be obtained in a very short period with a choice of power units, different gearboxes, air suspension and a high driving position just to mention some alternatives, all Dennis chasiss subsequently being given EEC Type Approval. It was to me all very encouraging, whereas today the British Leyland Motor Corporation and its various subsidiaries are no longer with us.

Mention is sometimes made of the Halifax, Hebble and Todmorden amalgamations and I oft times think about the way in which they went so well, in marked contrast to the much bigger enforced amalgamations of 1974.

Surprisingly, the one thing that I would like to be associated with has never yet been mentioned, namely the introduction of the Leicester Access Bus services. To see the way in which so many disabled persons who had been virtually home bound began to make use of the services, the way in which the volunteer 'Pushers' responded to a real need, and the various social gatherings that came to follow, was decidedly heart warming.

There are, of course, things I regret, top of the list being not to be firmly involved in the Gardner 5LXCT engine and Maxwell gearbox development work. I am sure that with tuning a useful saving in weight and fuel consumption could have been achieved, but with my quite sudden departure from Leicester and my interest in the project nothing of the sort was going to happen.

The other big doubt that used to occur to me was what would I have done if I had known that Tom Lord was going to resign as Director General as from 30th June 1976. Would I have stayed in Wakefield and fought for the top PTE job or would I still have applied earlier for the Leicester post? I am sure here the answer would have been in the affirmative but the even bigger regret is that John Timpson did not make his Plymouth approach two or three weeks earlier than he did. Had he done so there is no doubt that my career would have followed a very different path,

I must also regret the virtual elimination of the former municipal bus industry. This provided apprenticeships and openings for aspiring new entrants, as I was back in 1950, and offered the chance of working ones way, through energy and application, to the top of ones chosen profession. It also provided its resident population with high standard bus services at reasonable fares, not looking for the sort of dividend its shareholders might expect to receive, as seems all too frequent these days.

I must also mourn the passing of the former British commercial vehicle industry. However did we let it happen? I think back to my days with Seddon's when we despatched vehicles all round the world and again found opportunities for would-be apprentices and other staff members.

Now a trip down the motorway reveals haulage wedded to Swedish, German, French and Japanese vehicles in profusion with only the odd and elderly British-made truck putting in an appearance. It all makes me very very cross.

I must, though, set these latter thoughts aside and return to the theme of my opening paragraph in this 'Bigger Bit'.

It has been very gratifying to know that quite a number of bus enthusiasts have not forgotten me, have written to me in such complimentary terms, and continue to buy copies of volumes one and two. For all of these things I am truly grateful.

I hope, therefore, that this book provides. the reader with a pleasurable insight into what it was like to be involved in the later days of the municipal bus industry and in the earlier days of what came to replace it.

Geoffrey Hilditch. Torbay.
April 2013.

What might have been if....

Facing page, upper.
Plymouth Corporation had been an early user of Leyland Atlanteans, as had its neighbour Devon General. This Metro-Cammell-bodied example is from that first delivery in 1960, originally numbered 137 (TCO 537). It is still looking very smart in the Citybus livery, having been renumbered 7545.

Facing page, lower.
Some single-deckers were also to be found in the Plymouth fleet. In 1972 Leyland Nationals were purchased and No.26 (SCO 426L) has the famous Hoe for its backdrop.

Acknowledgements

As with the previous volume, the text of a work such as this needs to be profusely illustrated and here I must thank those friends who produced photographs from their files that I did not know existed, although in many instances I have no knowledge of who actually took them. The balance of the illustrations have come from my extensive personal collection or via the lenses of my various cameras. These have very kindly been supplemented by my friends at Venture Publications from the collections of Robert Edworthy, Harry Postlethwaite, Bob Rowe, Ian Stubbs and the Senior Transport Archive.

In addition to the foregoing I wish to thank the following old friends and colleagues who freely offered their help in producing additional information that was germane to this my story:-

Nigel Kirby — Producer of the Cynon Valley route maps.
Rhydian Williams — Former Chief Inspector Cynon Valley Transport.
John Smith — Former Managing Director Hestair Dennis.
Paul Gardner — Former Director L Gardner and Sons, Patricroft.
Geoff Lumb — Old friend and sole remaining Karrier owner.
Adam Mills — Former Deputy Chairman Drawlane Transport Group.
and last, but not least
Christopher Hilditch — Former Managing Director Midland Red North.